GOD MEANT IT FOR GOOD
Birthing A God-Sized Dream

The Prophetic Journey of Mark Danalis

By Mark Danalis
With Shara Lea Vithoulkas

Author's Note

To respect the privacy and well-being of individuals, certain names have been altered or withheld throughout this book.

Dedication

TO YESHUA

I want to take a moment to dedicate this book to Yeshua. It is overwhelming to me the reckless love You have for me when I didn't even know You. You had everything in heaven, but left it all behind and saw the joy (me) that was set before the cross, knowing that I was part of Your inheritance. Thank you for all the walls You pulled down and all the lies you tore down, as You faithfully delivered me out of darkness and into Your glorious light. All these years, You had been chasing me down and never gave up. I certainly didn't earn it, but You still fully gave Yourself away for me. I am eternally grateful that You have restored our relationship.

Your son,

Mark

Foreword by
Wayne Anderson

THE PROPHETIC JOURNEY OF MARK DANALIS

Be ready to be emotionally moved and even astounded by the story of life the way Mark Danalis lives it.

It is a great wonder to us how the end can start the beginning of something better than we could possibly imagine. The Holy One arrested Mark Danalis because Mark belonged to Him only. Arrested! Stopped in his tracks and was "rescued completely from the tyrannical rule of darkness" and was "translated into the Kingdom realm of His beloved Son. For in the Son, all our sins are canceled, and we have the release of redemption through His very blood." (Colossians 1:13-14 Passion Bible) Mark's life story is stunning to any everyday person, especially believers in Christ Jesus. Many think only of the miracles of being set free, but Mark sees the miracles in being caught red-handed and the blatant view of his sinful life decisions.

Life, as explained by Mark, is a learning process, and he has uniquely learned how "doing" must flow from "being." We are created as beings – beings in Christ Jesus. That which we do comes forth from our very being. Mark reveals to us in these pages that we cannot "do" in order to "be."

When looking into the complicated life of Joseph, son of Israel, Mark's real-life examples bring forth revelation. The traumas of Joseph's life became like a highway of holiness to the salvation of his inheritance and his family. Joseph was delivered from many complicated situations that could have remained debilitating traumas. However, the wonderful hand of Yahweh's directions held Joseph in His mighty grasp. The Holy One led Joseph into His salvation of Joseph and his inheritance.

It all starts not at the beginning of Mark's life. Life starts at the blunt-force trauma of loss. Seh Ah will never be forgotten. The heavenly fibers of her life (zoé) are in those who loved her and those who love because of her for uncountable generations to come. The Master said His final words on the cross, "Father, into Your hands I commit My Spirit." He is our model. The wealth of the Kingdom of Heaven is found herein. Seh Ah has so enriched the Danalis family as each loves and gives even as God so loves that He gave.

Personally, my tears come from the pain of such losses, but I know that my joy was conceived there in the midst of that pain.

In this book, Mark Danalis passionately uses the experiences of his own life to help others overcome their sin with the partnership of the Holy Spirit.

INTERNATIONAL
APOSTOLIC MINISTRIES

Wayne C. Anderson
Author, revivalist, apostolic father, preacher of Kingdom culture

Endorsements

Mark Danalis' book, *God Meant It For Good*, captured my attention from the first paragraph. Knowing and watching Mark grow in love with Jesus and the journey he made through his errors was a beautiful example of the restoration and forgiveness that Jesus produced in his life. I've known Mark to contend for the least, even when it has felt like nothing is working. He truly bears the marks of a man forgiven, but also the "marks of Jesus" that he has embraced in his own life. You will be blessed to join this journey with Mark that brings so much freedom.

- Danny Steyne, Mountain Of Worship (MOW) New England

Mark Danalis is a person I have known for less than a decade, but I have joy to write of his enthusiasm and love for our Savior, and his pursuit of truth and celebration of life!

Mark takes his walk with the Lord very seriously. I have personally witnessed Mark daily emulating things that he sees the Father do, and say the things he hears the Father say. I will share that I have also witnessed a growth curve in Mark that can only come through immersive measures in discipleship, prayer and study of The Word of God -- The Bible. He believes in others and I have found him to be very generous with his time, his heart, his faithfulness & loyalty to Christ Jesus and those who follow Him.

I believe this book will render very useful to the kingdom of God, and this generation in turning the hearts of the fathers to the children and bring many to the saving knowledge of our Lord and Savior Jesus Christ.

It is my honor to be able to recommend the investment of time to read and digest Mark's journey! May you allow the Holy Spirit

to speak to your heart and see where your journey may go after your investment of reading, by listening and seeking Him for more.
- Gina McDonald, Award winning William Raveis Agency &
"The American Dream" Reality TV Show Lead

It is my privilege to endorse Mark Danalis. His transformative journey unfolds through the pages of this book! You will be encouraged, equipped, and inspired to pursue true freedom in Christ. Mark is a man who lives in step with the Holy Spirit and walks with childlike faith. His consistent desire is to reflect the heart of his Heavenly Father. I sincerely hope this book leads you to have an encounter with the one true Living God!
- Josh Eldridge, Lead Pastor, Cornerstone Church

Jesus promises His disciples abundant life as we surrender our old lives to Him as Savior and start a new life with Him as Lord. Walking with Mark as a brother-in-the-Lord these last 13 years has given me a beautiful glimpse of a life committed to Jesus Christ. Mark has been on a fast-track with Jesus. With unwavering faith, Mark responds immediately to the leading of The Holy Spirit. This must be due to the time he spends daily in God's Word and prayer. He genuinely loves The Lord and loves people - and desires that they would also experience abundant life! You will laugh and rejoice as he shares his amazing life story. Hallelujah!
- Wolter and Tammy Webb-Witholt, "Beyond The Silence"

We had the joy of meeting Mark and becoming close friends at the time of his encounter with the Living God. Those were awesome days! Watching Mark's transformation into a 'new creation' was a genuine demonstration of God's redemptive power in a life completely submitted to Him. This book is an inspired testimony that will surely bear much fruit in the days to come.

- *Stuart and Sandra Gittleman, Engaging the Times*

There's nothing more compelling than the stories that bring us to Jesus. This is no exception. Mark's story is the stuff that movies are made of – but most of all the reminder that Jesus can free us from any prison we find ourselves in. He's just that good.

- *Michelle Schmidt, Artist and Educator*

Glory Be to God! What came to my mind reading my brother's testimony is that even when others look at our lives and think our lives are strange, they encounter the realness of our Lord. To witness the reformation in your own family member's heart, mind, and spirit is an inner work that only a living GOD can perform. Sherry and I have been praying for years for family members and friends to have this type of encounter (and for you, too). It brings me the greatest JOY to see Mark, his bride, his children and grandchildren saying 'yes' to Jesus is an incredible witness to a Sovereign Lord. I am so proud of the overcomer, the radical lover of the Lord that my brother has become. This testimony is a powerful witness when you apply faith and obedience to the written word of the Lord to your life. They were overcome by the power of their testimony."

- *Stephen and Sherry Danalis*
Families United Serving and Embracing (FUSE), Nehemiah House

God has blessed me with the privilege of meeting Mark on April 23, 2019. It is over this season of my life that I've been humbled countless times for his boundless love for Jesus. To simply say that Mark is a man of faith is not enough. It is his faith in Jesus Christ that makes him a visionary and a man of strong conviction, with a heart of sacrifice for others. Mark is a friend from beginning to end, no matter how painful the journey may be. He is a father to many, whose love is unconditional. He believes in God's blessings for his family and friends. He's a man of prayer and a teacher of obedience to God's Word. God has used him to strengthen the faith of many people. Mark gives God all the Honor, all the Glory, and only through the Power of the Holy Spirit is he now able to fulfill his Divine Destiny in God.

I know you will be blessed to read his book, as it will encourage you to endure life's trials and tribulations. Through his book, you'll get to know Mark Danalis, who God redeemed on life's battlefield, from fear and discouragement.

I am honored to call Mark my brother in Christ.

- Giuseppe Joseph Bono

"Unless a seed falls into the ground and dies, it remains only a single seed. But if it dies, it will produce many seeds." I see my friend Mark as a seed that has gone into the ground and has died to his old life. His powerful story will produce much fruit in the Kingdom of God. Mark's testimony of the resurrected life will surely inspire others as they read his book.

- Ray Bugnacki, co-founder of The Mem Gathering

TABLE OF CONTENTS

Chapter 1
Facing Years in Prison

BREAKDOWN BEFORE BREAKTHROUGH

Lou Engle: "God had a dream and wrapped your body around you.... Every life is a story. Don't bail out on your storyline. In the bad times, don't get bitter. In the end, God doesn't write any bad novels.... There are moments in history when a door for massive change opens. Great revolutions for good or for evil occur by these openings. It is in these "openings" times that key men and women, even entire generations, risk everything to become that **hinge of history**, that pivotal point that determines which way the door will swing."

A HINGE OF HISTORY IN MY LIFE:
KNOCK FROM THE POLICE

April 11, 2008 was a hinge of history in my own life. That day a door swung wide in my destiny forever. It was a day that will live in infamy. I was arrested. I was busted for my marijuana drug deals. Sometimes your world comes crashing down because of your own wrong choices. Life as I knew it completely stopped. God is so rich

1

in mercy and slow to anger that He apprehended me even in my sin. It was my breakdown right before God brought His breakthrough.

Friday at one o'clock in the afternoon someone pounded loudly on the door of my East Longmeadow house. I had spent the day baking homemade biscuits for strawberry shortcakes. I wanted to surprise my family with tickets to Cirque du Soleil and a decadent dessert spread. I come from a big Greek family where we love to eat. I think eating delicious meals should be a sixth love language.

But then came the knock. Over the sound of the KitchenAid beater whipping the cream for the freshly cut red strawberries. The fresh smell of hot biscuits baking in the oven filled the air, but there was no way to ignore the pound at the door. "I will be right there!"

My hands were covered in flour and sticky with dough. I was so cocky and arrogant. My identity was masked as a successful businessman and drug dealer. I actually believed I was untouchable. Everything I had done up until this point in life was completely under the radar. I thought I was invincible... unbeatable... even unstoppable. But pride comes before the fall. And that fall came with the knock. A knock which changed my life. My kingdom came crashing down.

"I will be right there. Hang on."

The pounding crescendoed like the beating of my heart. But what awaited me on the other side of my front door forever brought me to my knees....

NOWHERE TO RUN AND NOWHERE TO HIDE

I opened the door to find close to a dozen DEA, US Marshals, local and state police were awaiting my open door. Even the IRS came to greet me! Drug hounds sniffed ferociously around my house. Above, the helicopters hovered and whirred, drowning out the sound of my racing heart.

I was 46 years old and had spent my life never getting caught. No police record. No criminal record. I was able to hold a New York poker face.

They barged in when I opened the door and said in a loud forceful voice, "What are you doing?" My adrenaline surged but I was able to maintain composure. Almost as if I was welcoming them to come sit down at my dining room table and enjoy my biscuits, I smiled and said, "Come in. I am making strawberry shortcakes."

Looking around, his voice calmed and he said "You really are making strawberry shortcakes."

THE RIGHT TO REMAIN SILENT

They read me my Miranda rights. I had watched enough cop shows on TV to understand my rights to remain silent. Anything I said could and would be used against me in the court of law. As the handcuffs cut into my wrist and restricted my freedom, I knew I would be locked in a cold cell. The hard back of the dining chair kept me sitting upright as my spirits fell.

I looked out the window and watched as all my possessions were hauled off one by one. The cops carted off my $70,000 corvette, $35,000 Ford Explorer, $25,000 Indian motorcycle, $25,000 boat, $15,000 snowmobiles and trailer. They repossessed all my assets. They looked like ants scurrying away with a food supply for the queen ant. My life's loot disappeared before my eyes. Deep down, I had this uncanny relief.

IT'S FINALLY OVER

"But the Lord said to him, 'Go, for he is a chosen vessel of Mine to bear My name before Gentiles, kings, and the children of Israel. For I will show him how many things he must suffer for My name's sake.'

"And Ananias went his way and entered the house; and laying his hands on him he said, "Brother Saul, the Lord Jesus, who appeared to you on the road as you came, has sent me that you may receive your sight and be filled with the Holy Spirit." Immediately there fell from his eyes something like scales, and he received his sight at once; and he arose and was baptized. So when he had received food, he was strengthened. Then Saul spent some days with the disciples at Damascus." (Acts 9:15-19)

"It is over. It is finally over." A weird sense of relief washed over me, as this deep knowing permeated my soul. I had been running for so long. I love the quote from Jim Elliot: "He is no fool who gives what he cannot keep to gain that which he cannot lose."

The truth is I am pretty stubborn. I know now it was God's mercy to help me lose everything to gain Him. I had this odd sense that a spiritual veil had finally been ripped off my eyes. It was just like this passage in Acts 9 when God restored Paul's sight. Since I had received Jesus as my Lord and Savior three months earlier, the strongholds in my life had only gotten worse. I was struggling with what the Bible describes as a reprobate mind. Just like Apostle Paul had scales fall off his eyes after he was blinded, God was opening my eyes, as if for the first time. Light was creeping into the cobwebs of a double-minded life of depravity.

It had only been three months since I had surrendered my life to Jesus. That was another day I will never forget. It was the day my brother and his wife buried their beautiful toddler who they had adopted from Korea. There had been a tragic accident at their house that resulted in her death. Could anything be more traumatic? But it was the excruciating, life-altering pain which brought me to Jesus. None of us would ever be the same.

After the accident, our fun and lively Greek family hit rock bottom. As we descended into this abyss of unimaginable tragedy, God gently stooped down to rescue me. The very day she was buried was the day that I found Jesus. Her seed is what gave me life.

As a baby Christian, I had this gnawing conviction that I could no longer straddle between two worlds. Six months earlier, I had also gone through a traumatic divorce.

THE VEIL WAS LIFTED

It was as if the spiritual veil that Satan had masked me with was finally ripped off. I had been incapable of walking away from my sinful life on my own. As strange as that seemed, I felt like The Father was checkmating me, mercifully backing me into a corner where the only way out was to look up. It was as if He was gently assuring my heart that in losing the world, I was gaining Him. A peace that transcends all understanding washed over me. I had felt like I had been fumbling in a dark room for twenty years, and my arrest was like someone mercifully turning on the lights. I was lost. Now, I was found. What was I thinking all this time?

My phone started ringing off the hook, breaking my dazed look. I watched my possessions being hauled off like a Monopoly board being cleared. My family was waiting for the Cirque du Soleil show. I could not answer. The police had scoured every inch of the house.

For the past twenty years, I'd grown marijuana in the State of Massachusetts. I always had a green thumb even as a little boy. At ten years old, I started my first garden growing bright fresh tomatoes for my parents and brothers. Everything I touched turned green and as an adult, gold.

On the other side of town, I had transformed my commercial garage into an indoor grow facility for pot. I had to hide my illegal business so I stealthily put in generators, so even the electric bill would not reveal my illegal business.

I listened as the police radioed back and forth, "Go to the garage now! Stat!"

THE GARAGE GROW ROOM

My heart stopped. No longer could I run or hide. The cops hit the jackpot. I could not control anything. You would have thought I would have dreaded being arrested, and facing jail time, but I was in this bubble of grace. A deep peace guided me like a compass pointing me due North. Somehow, I knew it was the loving kindness of My Perfect Father who loved me so much He would not leave me to myself, perishing in my depravity. It was His kindness to lead me to repentance.

One of the cops put me in the back of the police car and drove me to the station where I was put into a jail cell overnight.

The local police station jail cell was humble. An old, cold, stainless-steel toilet without a lid awaited me. There was only a stiff, cold bed in the jail cell. The light was on 24/7, so time blurred under the constant fluorescent light. I remember lying on the mattress like a bed of nails, and my whole world was swimming before my eyes.

The Holy Spirit guides us to all Truth. Truth is a Person. His name is Jesus. And in His lovingkindness, He was allowing me to face the consequence of my actions. I had this sudden urge to pray.

Just as Adam had tried to hide behind trees and fig leaves after he disobeyed, I knew I had no place to run but into the loving arms of My Father. It was time to fall back into the arms of the One who knew me best, yet loved me most. Jesus was the Only way. He was the Truth. He was the light.

*Even as a young boy, I was growing fresh vegetables
for my parents and brothers.*

Chapter 2
Surrendering to Jesus
in a Jail Cell

The lights in the jail cell flickered like the conviction growing in my soul. I knew that this was all my doing. I knew I was wrong. The only way now was to kneel down low.

The cold hard floor of the jail cell transformed into a sanctuary of surrender. As a baby Christian, I was like a newborn crying out with simple syllables. I knew I was dependent upon my Abba Father to survive. I had hit my breakdown: and my father would use my breakdown for my eternal breakthrough.

"Lord, forgive me. I know this is all my fault. I know I deserve what is coming, but please give me a graceful, soft landing."

I wish I could say that I felt something when I prayed, but I felt like my words bounced off the ceiling. This prayer of surrender was made in blind faith. Jesus is the ultimate advocate. He is the Judge above all Judges, and what He determines in the Courts of Heaven precedes any temporal judgments.

"God works all things together for the good of those who love God and are called according to his purpose." (Romans 8:28). The Lord had used the pain of my niece's death to break up the soil of my hard heart. Only God could win in a tragedy. God is with each of us in the midst of

all despair and hopelessness. He is Immanuel - God with us. Even when we do not know where we are, or how we got to that dark place, He is right there in the middle of it. He is the Light of the World. There is no shadow of turning in Him. There is no shifting or darkness in His Marvelous light. The darker the world gets, the brighter He shines.

His light crashed into my darkness. I once was blind but now I could see. I once was lost. Now I was found. After that simple prayer, I was able to curl up on the hard bed and await what the morning would bring.

BAIL WAS SET

"I am not supposed to be here." Rang through my thoughts. But deep down, I knew I was guilty, so I kept my right to remain silent. The next morning bail was set for $20,000.

I called a friend of mine who came and bailed me out. I was released to go home to wait for the arraignment in court.

A NEW DAY DAWNING

I remember the sound of the jail cell opening. I remember the feel of the sunshine's warmth pouring onto my face, and the smell of the fresh April grass. I felt such deep freedom fill my soul. I cannot imagine how others live their lives in prison.

One night in jail was all I could take. That isolation was an invitation into divine intimacy, birthing destiny, changing history.

Saturday morning after I was bailed out, I walked out of jail as a new man. Even though I had the impending doom of court awaiting Monday morning, I felt free on the inside.

Sometimes we have to lose everything to appreciate what we do have. I left that jail cell transformed. Just like Paul and Silas worshiped and God sent an earthquake to open the prison doors, I surrendered my life to Jesus even when I was guilty and God heard my prayers. What goes up always comes down. God always answers prayer. His arm is not too short to save nor His ears too dull to hear.

HEADLINES AND TV STAR

I became a TV star overnight as the local television station broadcast my arrest (I have included the news article at the end of this chapter). I was headline news. The humiliation was overwhelming, especially with my family and friends. It is interesting to see who is there for you when you lose everything. My new Christian brothers from my church contacted me to lift me up and support me. They reassured me that God still had a great plan for me. But how could God have a plan for a sinner like me? How could He ever work this for good? The spirit of depression covered me like a familiar down comforter snuffing out the sunlight of hope. Was my life over? Was there no hope? God, are You even there?

The court date had been set and my case had been docketed for early Monday morning. I quickly hired a criminal defense attorney, Vincent A. Bongiorni, who had garnered the respect of the community. Everything was happening so quickly, I only got to meet him in person at court. He knew how to play the strings of the court system like an expert. I turned to him and said, "We've got to talk."

I had so many assets that I was nervous they would be repossessed. I had $250,000 just sitting in a bank account, and I was worried that my accounts would be frozen. He advised me to move the money.

That afternoon, I went to my local bank to draw out a cashier's check. I had grown up in this little town. The sleepy community of Longmeadow, Massachusetts, had a small town feel of "Cheers" where everyone knew your name.

As I tried to withdraw my money, the bank teller grew anxious. His eyes darted back and forth between the computer screen and me. He left to consult with his manager and returned with sweat beading down his face. He looked at me and sheepishly said, "There is someone at the other branch right now withdrawing this money."

The IRS and US Marshal had beat me to the punch. In a moment, I lost everything. I left the bank empty handed and called my attorney. He said, "When they catch someone doing something wrong, they think they can just take everything."

Mission accomplished. They took everything except my credit card they left on the table.

MY COUSIN VINNY

Vinny had a strong reputation for a reason. He soon discovered that the police had illegally used a tracking device that was connected to a cell phone on my car. Vinny knew we could get the case thrown out of court because of it. The prosecuting team got nervous, so they pushed to have the case escalated quickly to a federal level where they are more forgiving on the prosecutor's side because they didn't want to lose the case.

I realized I would have to make an oath and "swear to God" on the Bible in court. After that simple prayer of surrender in the jail cell, I knew I could no longer lie. It was time to come clean. There was nowhere to go but to Him. I told my attorney that I could not lie in court. I wanted to come clean and make a deal. He encouraged me that the best way forward was to make the deal, not to fight and that both parties could walk away from the bargaining table feeling as if everyone had won. I was done fighting. I was done lying. It was time to repent and change my ways.

GOD WHO IS RICH IN MERCY

Since the case had been escalated to a federal level, a guilty verdict would incur greater prison time. If you have over 100 plants, it is a federal offense. The FBI said I had 103 plants when I thought I only had 97 plants.

The detectives went around the community in an effort to gather as much information as they could in order to strengthen their case.

When we confess our sins, God is faithful and righteous to forgive us of our sins. I was guilty as charged. I should have done time in jail. But I had made a deal with God. If God spared my life, my life belonged to Him and Him alone.

Vinny was shocked as the FBI needed final approval on the deal we had from the leadership in Boston. A deal was struck! There was no jail time and I owed $650,000 and had to serve probation for three years. He excitedly said, "I cannot believe they even agreed to this!" He said there are other people whose crimes were much less, yet they had to do time.

God did have a plan and a purpose for my life. God is rich in mercy and slow to anger. He is the Ultimate God of the second chance. He is the God of the underdog, and the comeback kid. I was a baby Christian who had just met Jesus, but He spared me from prison time and gave me a fresh start to serve Him. Now, I was simply a bond servant to Jesus.

In addition to the various assets the police had already seized, I owned duplexes and commercial investment properties which were my source of income. The Lord brought me to a point of sweet surrender knowing that if I lost my rental income, He would still take care of me. He was My Provider. I surrendered the properties to God in prayer. Everything we own belongs to Him anyway! The Father saw my change of heart and my trust in Him.

JOY UNSPEAKABLE FULL OF GLORY

During one of the key negotiating meetings we went to, I remember the officer asked me, "How do you feel? Do you want to kill yourself?" I simply responded, "I have joy!"

I was able to give him that answer because each day I spent hours at God's feet in prayer and reading His Holy Word. I had witnessed how my sister-in-law got through the unimaginable loss of her daughter by being in God's presence and His Word. As I faced the stress of a police record and fines, I needed supernatural strength.

It was by the grace of God that the FBI would allow me to keep my duplexes and my investment properties as a source of income. Eighteen months later, I was able to cash out all my investments and pay off my $650,000 debt owed to the government for money laundering and the drugs.

I still had three years' probation to serve. It was when I hit rock bottom that I met my Eternal Rock and Savior Jesus Christ. This was my road to Damascus experience. Here is the article on the arrest:

Big Agawam Drug Bust Pays Dividends
For Western Massachusetts Law Enforcement Agencies
By Jack Flynn | jflynn@repub.com

DRUG MONEY DISTRIBUTION

U.S. Attorney Carmen Ortiz this week announced the distribution of $650,000 in forfeited money seized in a 2008 drug raid in Agawam. Here are the agencies which received funds:

Northwestern District Attorney
U.S. Drug Enforcement Agency – $130,000
Northampton Police Department
Easthampton Police Department
Hampden District Attorney
West Springfield Police Department
Springfield Police Department
Internal Revenue Service
Chicopee Police Department
Holyoke Police Department

SPRINGFIELD – A huge marijuana bust in Agawam has yielded a $650,000 payoff for area law enforcement agencies.

In pleading guilty to running a sophisticated marijuana growing operation down the street from the Six Flags New England amusement park last year, Mark J. Danalis, of Agawam, agreed to surrender cash and assets from the business, including a 2006 Corvette and a 20-foot Stingray boat.

The deal, authorized by the U.S. Attorney's Office, capped a two-year investigation that began with the Northwestern District Attorney's office and the Northampton Police Department and eventually involved eight other law enforcement agencies across the region.

U.S. Attorney Carmen M. Ortiz came to Springfield this week to praise the teamwork of the participating agencies and announce the distribution of the funds.

"Forfeiture is a very powerful enforcement tool used against a wide spectrum of crimes, including drug trafficking," said Ortiz on Wednesday, adding she was "delighted" to award the funds to the 10 agencies responsible for the seizure.

In April, 2008, state police seized 103 marijuana plants and two generators during a raid on the marijuana growing operation at 1779 Main Street. Danalis, an East Longmeadow resident at the time, was arrested at the site.

Police also seized a 2006 Corvette, a 2004 Ford Explorer, a 2002 Indian Chief motorcycle, a Yamaha 660 Quad, a 20-foot Stingray boat, and two Arctic Cat snowmobiles from Danalis as proceeds of the sale of marijuana.

In January, Danalis was given three years' probation after pleading guilty to possession with intent to distribute marijuana, and ordered to forfeit cash and assets totaling $650,000.

The Northwestern District Attorney's office received the largest among, $207,677, and the remainder was divided among other federal, regional and municipal law enforcement agencies, including police departments in Northampton, Easthampton, West Springfield, Springfield, Chicopee and Holyoke.

Renee L. Steese, assistant district attorney for Northwest district attorney's office, said the conviction and forfeiture were the result of a long and expensive investigation. "There were lengthy surveillance's and essentially used leather-on-the-pavement old fashion police work," Steese said.

The office has not received the money yet, and has not decided how to use it. Generally, money seized in drug raids is used to finance future investigations, Steese said.

Northampton Detective Lt. Kenneth J. Watson said his department often uses seized drug proceeds to pay for new equipment, training and overtime for surveillance work. "This is a significant amount for us. It should (last) for a while," he said.

With or without the financial bonus, Watson said, solving the case was its own reward. "We all worked well together, and we brought someone to justice," he said.

The Lord said I heard you praying the Lord's prayer
and I delivered you from the evil one.

Chapter 3
From Pit to Prison

If there's a character in the Bible I most relate to, it's Joseph, Jacob's beloved eleventh son, firstborn with his favorite wife Rachel. Joseph was born to Rachel after many years of infertility. She named her son Joseph, *Yosef* in Hebrew, which means "increase," expressing her wish that God grant her an additional son.

The Bible Story of Joseph, from the Book of Genesis 37-50, is one of heroic redemption and forgiveness. He was a dreamer of God's impossible dreams, but there was a lifelong process preparing Joseph to have the character to carry his God dreams to pass. The story of Joseph, the son of Jacob who was called Israel, is a vivid representation of the great truth that all things work together for good to those who love God. (Romans 8:28.)

WORDS CREATE WORLDS

"These are the generations of Jacob. Joseph, being seventeen years old, was feeding the flock with his brethren; and the lad was with the sons of Bilhah, and with the sons of Zilpah, his father's wives: and Joseph brought to his father their evil report. Now Israel loved Joseph more than all his children, because he was the son of his old age: and he made him a coat of many colors. And

when his brethren saw that their father loved him more than all his brethren, they hated him, and could not speak peaceably unto him." (Genesis 37:2-4 emphasis mine)

I think I relate to Joseph as he was quite arrogant when he was young. We have to be careful of what we speak out into existence, we want to speak forth blessings and not curses. In Genesis, it reports that Joseph had "L'shon Hara" - a continual flow of evil speech or tattle-telling. Joseph was immature, but also arrogant and ignorant. For example, when Joseph reported having dreams of his brothers, represented by the stars and moon bowing before him, their jealousy of Joseph grew into action leading them to ultimately sell him into slavery. Because I had a lifetime of success, God had to humble and mature me just like He did with Joseph.

The Bible warns us to watch our words. A right prophecy spoken at the wrong time is a wrong word. I love Ephesians 4:29-30 in The Passion Translation (TPT): "*And never let ugly or hateful words come from your mouth, but instead let your words become beautiful gifts that encourage others; do this by speaking words of grace to help them. The Holy Spirit of God has sealed you in Jesus Christ until you experience your full salvation. So never grieve the Spirit of God or take for granted his holy influence in your life.*"

Kris Vallotton preaches how our tests are for our testimony and our mess is for our message. One day, Jacob instructed Joseph to visit his brothers in Shechem, where they were tending their sheep for their father. Little did Jacob know that this would be the last time he would see his favorite, beloved son, until their reunion a long twenty-two years later.

PIT TO POTIPHAR'S HOUSE TO PRISON TO PALACE

"Now when they saw him afar off, even before he came near them, they conspired against him to kill him. Then they said to one another, 'Look, this dreamer is coming! Come therefore, let us now kill him and cast him into some pit; and we shall say, 'Some wild beast has devoured him.' We shall see what will become of his dreams!" (Genesis 37:18-20)

Seizing their chance, the brothers threw the unsuspecting Joseph into a waterless pit. A short while later, his brothers sold Joseph into slavery with traders. He was eventually brought to Egypt, where he was sold to Potiphar, one of King Pharaoh's ministers. He had over a twenty-year journey from pit to Potiphar's house to prison to palace.

WHEN IT THUNDERS, GOD IS BOWLING

I once asked my mom if heaven was real. She responded "Yes. And when it is thundering out, God's bowling." That was the extent of what I knew about God – heaven was a distant bowling alley with a man in the sky – like a far-off Santa Claus. I knew God was real but I did not know Him in an intimate way. Growing up in a tight Greek family, I had three beloved brothers. Growing up as one of four boys was almost like being in a pack of wolves. Together we learned the art of survival.

We all attended the Greek Orthodox Church where my dad was the President. It is not an exaggeration to say it was all Greek to me! I chose not to engage because I did not speak Greek. All the services were in Greek/English, and I did not understand a word. The pews were filled with many precious Greek grandmas who

23

read their Bibles, but all I could do was sleep through the services. I grew up with no understanding of the gospel. I was a church attender but not a true believer or follower of Jesus.

A CALL THAT BECAME AN ETERNAL WAKE UP CALL

My brother was my best friend and the best man at my wedding. We lived ten minutes apart. Early one morning in January 2008, my older brother called to tell me that there was a tragic accident and that our younger brother's adopted daughter Seh Ah had passed away last night. The reality of the news shook through the core of me like the epicenter of an earthquake. "Is this for real? Am I caught in a nightmare? Would someone just wake me up?"

C.S. Lewis said, "Pain is God's megaphone to rouse a deaf world." God was screaming to me through my niece's death. Our world turned upside down.

UNLESS A GRAIN OF WHEAT FALLS TO THE GROUND AND DIES...

"Listen carefully: Unless a grain of wheat is buried in the ground, dead to the world, it is never any more than a grain of wheat. But if it is buried, it sprouts and reproduces itself many times over. In the same way, anyone who holds on to life just as it is destroys that life. But if you let it go, reckless in your love, you'll have it forever, real and eternal." (John 12:24 The Message)

Seh Ah was buried five days later on Martin Luther King Junior's birthday. Little did I know that on the day of her burial, God would use her death as a seed to help me to eternal life.

The Memorial took place at Bethany Assembly of God in Agawam, MA. The church was packed as the news of Seh Ah's death had rocked our community. Hundreds of people packed into the pews, and my family sat in the front row. I watched as my brother courageously stepped to the stage, leaning into the pulpit to help bear his weight as he delivered the eulogy. (I've included it at the end of the chapter.)

He held himself together. All eyes were glued to him. You could hear a pin drop. His lips quivered, but every word and phrase was crafted by The Father Himself. My brother's words gripped everyone's attention, as the power and presence of God filled the sanctuary.

It was one of the most powerful experiences of my life. As soon as my brother finished, I thought, "He did not write that. That is not how my brother writes." I held back hot tears from splashing down my face. It was as if my brother took my niece gently by **her** hand and walked **her** spirit home to heaven, fully releasing her from his arms and care to the loving arms of her Heavenly Father. I sat in awe. The presence of God gripped everyone. Even to this day, many remind my brother and sister-in-law how his words forever changed their lives. My sister-in-law later explained how the Holy Spirit had spoken directly through him. This is the eulogy he shared on the day of the funeral:

SEH AH: OUR ANGEL ON LOAN

I want to praise God for all the blessings he has bestowed upon my family all my life. I cannot stand here on my own strength but only the strength the Lord has given me to do so.

Everything we have is on loan. We own nothing. We come into this world with nothing and leave with nothing.

No one, no one is promised tomorrow. So please love one another like there is no tomorrow. The greatest commodity we have is LOVE... to receive it and to give it. Why the Lord only loaned us this angel for two years... we'll know in time or when we get to glory. Her seed will blossom.

I would say to my father only the good die young... and you and I aren't going anywhere soon.... He'd say speak for yourself.

Seh Ah was an angel to all that met her. I believe God preserved Seh Ah before the world could perverse her soul.

Who's more welcomed into the Lord's arms than the innocence of a beautiful child? She is not accountable.

But we here that have heard of the Lord and His son are all accountable for our sinful nature. Don't weep for us but weep for the one that does not have a relationship with God and His son. It's the only way to true peace.

Don't let Seh Ah's death be the end of hope but the beginning of faith.

My home stands firm as a family of Christ... whoever believes in God's son will have everlasting life. The only way I can see my daughter again is to believe in Him and do my best to strive towards the likeness of Jesus.

If you don't read and believe in God's word... you don't believe in the promise of a place called heaven.

God does not break promises.

Saturday morning... our faith was met with your prayers. My wife and I woke up and talked about Wednesday's tragic events all morning. The pain was lifted from both of us. We looked at each other and knew we had received the promise of the Holy spirit, the comforter which Jesus promised his Father would send after his death.

We had PEACE. It's been undeniable. A miracle! How can we humanly... possibly have a moment's peace in a time like this.

Thank you, Lord.

If God can lift this pain... Anything is possible if you believe and trust in Him.

This tragedy does not bring a wedge between God and my family.

We stand arm in arm in God's fruitful plan with our lives as we strive towards Him as one. The video presented today shows all the joy she brought to our lives.

My daughter is one of the most beautiful souls I ever knew. I love my wife and boys more than ever. I love all of you.

As we were driving here my wife read to me Philippians 4:7 (NIV): "And the peace of God, which transcends all understanding, will guard your hearts and your minds in Christ Jesus." Thank you all for being here.

Thinking of God as a distant far off Santa Claus.

Chapter 4
Meeting My Best Friend Jesus

My sister-in-law's cousin Sarah had a heart to sow a financial seed for my niece's adoption from Korea. Sarah has four boys and so she wanted to help adopt this baby girl. Her name was Seh Ah, which means "beautiful."

As soon as Sarah got the call about my niece's death, the Holy Spirit told her to fly in right away and be a "vessel of love" to radically minister to our family in our time of need. The day after the death, Sarah jumped on a plane and flew across the country. The Lord had spoken to her so clearly about how to minister to our family. She was the one who encouraged my brother to share his heart in his weakness, because people were coming with open hearts and it was going to be a harvest of souls.

MONDAY, JANUARY 21, 2008: MLK JUNIOR DAY

After the funeral, the family gathered at my brother's house. I was still in shock at how God had spoken through my brother. That was not how my brother talks. Through tenderness and tears, he spoke about his baby girl who had been an angel on loan. Because Sarah encouraged him to be bold even in his brokenness, my brother fully shared his heart with his eulogy. We were all in awe of how God had spoken through him.

I asked my sister-in-law how that was even possibly my brother? She sweetly smiled and said how that was the Holy Spirit sharing through him.

A VESSEL OF LOVE

"If you want to change the world, go home and love your family...." (Mother Teresa) *"Love begins at home, and it is not how much we do, but how much love we put in the action that we do."* (Mother Teresa)

The love of God poured out of Sarah so profoundly. Like a puppy dog, I lapped up every word and followed her around the house, eager to hear every nugget of wisdom and revelation. She ministered to people one by one and in groups. I wanted to confess my sins and I kept telling her, "But, you don't know what I did! You don't know what I did!" I felt that my past would disqualify me from salvation. If she knew the truth about me, would she still love me? Would God still love me? She kept reassuring me that nothing could separate me from the love of God and Jesus is for everyone. She explained that Jesus always wins. This news felt too good to be true.

"Who shall separate us from the love of Christ? Shall tribulation, or distress, or persecution, or famine, or nakedness, or peril, or sword? As it is written: 'For Your sake we are killed all day long; We are accounted as sheep for the slaughter.' Yet in all these things we are more than conquerors through Him who loved us. For I am persuaded that neither death nor life, nor angels nor principalities nor powers, nor things present nor things to come, nor height nor depth, nor any other created thing, shall be able to separate us from the love

of God which is in Christ Jesus our Lord." (Romans 8:35-39 emphasis, mine)

I imagine when Jesus walked the earth there was a circle of followers including his disciples and children who clung to His every word. I clung onto Sarah's every word in probably the same way Peter, John and James followed the Lamb wherever He would go.

MY SPIRITUAL BIRTHDAY

That night, we gathered in my brother's office. Waves of liquid love flowed out of every word Sarah spoke. How did she love like that? What made her so different? Why did she carry this joy unspeakable – full of glory? She was the hands and feet of Jesus to me. God worked so powerfully through her.

I heard the gospel message for the first time in my life. People talk about a "God shaped hole" that only The Father can fill. I had an overwhelming desire to know God more, but I honestly had never really heard someone talk to God, or even pray. I got on my knees in front of my family, and prayed the sinner's prayer. I surrendered my life to Jesus. Sarah sang over me at the top of her lungs like a birthday party. Worship was her warfare. She was so lost in love and it was as if heaven and earth were serenading me on my spiritual birthday.

She laughed and told me that the angels were rejoicing. She explained that Jesus had waited my entire life for that moment.

THE BIBLE IS THE ONLY LIVING BOOK
IN THE WORLD

God sees it all. He never wastes our pain or our past. One of my favorite names for God is El Roi which is what Hagaar calls God in the desert after Abraham banishes her and Ishmael. When God provided a well of water in her wilderness, she looked up from her abandonment and declared: "El Roi. He is the God Who Sees Me!" God saw each of our family members and met each of the Danalis family in such a unique way.

Sarah profoundly ministered to my sister-in-law who was crippled with grief. In the face of unimaginable pain, my sister-in-law was set on fire by the power and love of God. All we could do was watch her burn as she sought God like never before. I witnessed the Word of God transform my sister-in-law into a tower of strength. I would go over morning, noon and night and see her reading God's word. She would never put down the Bible. Months later when I was in prison, I remembered her testimony and followed this example. It was not antidepressants or therapy which healed her. The Word of God changed her life.

What is so interesting is three months later, on the exact day I was arrested, God led Sarah to fly in again! God had powerfully used this woman and knitted our lives together. In the months following my salvation and arrest I spent my time really pressing in to know the Lord like never before.

MOLDED IN THE MUNDANE:
MAN LOOKS AT OUTWARD APPEARANCE,
GOD LOOKS AT THE HEART

The story of Joseph brings such comfort to my soul. Have you ever felt you were thrown in a pit? Have you experienced being betrayed by your family? Have you been wrongly accused? Joseph was a dreamer who experienced all of this.

We love to live in an instant society. But God is all about process. Daniel was 80 years old when he received his first dream. Moses was 40 years old when he left the Pharaoh's palace in Egypt, and it was 40 years later that he had the burning bush experience. God has to deliver us first to make us a deliverer. The story of Joseph encourages my heart so much as there was such a purpose to the pain.

PURPOSE IN THE PAIN

Joseph dreamed an impossible dream. Joseph's name means "May God bring the increase." Even though he was a shepherd in the land of Canaan just like Moses and David, God had a calling on him but had to mold him in the mundane. Joseph went from the waterless pit, to Potiphar's house to prison, but he refused to stay stuck. Sometimes we forget that there is purpose in our pain. The way I pushed through the depression of the crushing events was by pressing into God. I devoured The Word like food.

LOVING THE HELL OUT OF ME

A few couples from my church loved the hell out of me! God handpicked a family of friends to walk with me. They would lay hands on me and pray for so long. I remember being a bit overwhelmed at how long they wanted to pray for me, but every time I would leave refreshed and transformed. How much we need God, but how much we also need His family!

Sarah continued to be a spiritual mentor to me. To this day, she is a modern-day revivalist who restores so many women to their God given identity and destiny. Revelations 19 promises that the Spirit of Prophecy is the testimony of Jesus. Her life has become a testimony revealing the beauty of Jesus.

In the years that followed, she encouraged me that my life would be like a modern-day Joseph. God promises us that the Father will work all things together for the good of those who love him and are called according to his purposes. (Romans 8:28) even what the enemy intended for evil (Genesis 50:20).

AMAZING GRACE BY JOHN NEWTON

Amazing grace how sweet the sound
That saved a wretch like me
I once was lost, but now I'm found
Was blind but now I see
'Twas grace that taught my heart to fear
And grace my fears relieved
How precious did that grace appear
The hour I first believed
Through many dangers, toils, and snares

I have already come
This grace that brought me safe thus far
And grace will lead me home
When we've been here ten thousand years
Bright, shining as the sun
We've no less days to sing, God's praise
Than when we first begun
Amazing grace how sweet the sound
That saved a wretch like me
I once was lost, but now I'm found
Was blind but now I see

Love came down and rescued me.
(painting by Elaine Danalis)

Chapter 5
The Power of Purity:
The Test with Potiphar's Wife

When Satan tempts men to commit one sin, he teaches them to try to conceal the one sin with another sin, which only increases the iniquity. For example, maybe he lures us to hide theft or murder by lying. When we cover sin, we shall not prosper long. In the end, the truth always comes out.

WHEN WE WALK IN THE LIGHT

When we walk in His light, sin has no power over us. Light shines brightest in the darkness. I have had a journey of overcoming temptations. Two keys I have learned is to walk in godly submission and find consistent accountability in sexual purity.

Joseph's brothers kept their sin hidden. Their hearts were strangely hardened by the deceitfulness of sin. They even lied to their father Jacob who refused to be comforted. Years passed and they were buried in this secret sin that their father's deep grief was their fault.

POWER COMES FROM PURITY

"As for you, son of man, you've become quite the talk of the town. Your people meet on street corners and in front of their houses and say, 'Let's go hear the latest news from GOD.' They show up, as people tend to do, and sit in your company. They listen to you speak, but don't do a thing you say. They flatter you with compliments, but all they care about is making money and getting ahead. To them you're merely entertainment—a country singer of sad love songs, playing a guitar. They love to hear you talk, but nothing comes of it. But when all this happens—and it is going to happen!—they'll realize that a prophet was among them." (Ezekiel 33:30-33 The Message, MSG)

From Joseph's journey, we see how important it is to truly heed the Word of the Lord and steward our prophetic promises. For Joseph to fulfill his calling, it required not just the gifts of the spirit, but the fruit of the spirit described in Galatians 5:22-23: *"But the fruit of the Spirit is love, joy, peace, long-suffering, kindness, goodness, faithfulness, gentleness and self-control."* We see these fruits, especially long-suffering, in the purity and integrity of Joseph's character. Joseph had impeccable integrity.

Man tends to measure success with numbers, but God looks for depth and not breadth. The Father builds big people – not just big churches.

Remember Noah! After 120 years of preaching a clear word to repent, only eight people entered Noah's ark. If Noah had measured his success by numbers, he would have been depressed. But he walked in a fear of the Lord and lived a righteous life.

We have lost the fear of the Lord in Western Christianity and all too often cower to a fear of man instead. What I love about Joseph was that he walked in the fear of the Lord and walked in integrity. He lived before an Audience of One – even when he was mistreated.

38

REFUSING POTIPHAR'S WIFE

Joseph was able to deny Potiphar's wife's sexual advances, as he refused to sleep with her. It was his purity which set him apart. Consecration is a powerful weapon! Just like Joseph drew close to God who molded his character, we can only walk in a measure of authority to the degree we maintain sexual morality. God used the pain and suffering to call Joseph higher. He became so trustworthy that he was even promoted to his position as viceroy.

MY TESTIMONY OF OVERCOMING SEXUAL ADDICTION AFTER THE DIVORCE

Soon after my divorce, I thought I was a free man, but that was really an illusion. A gnawing, aching hunger -- a God-shaped void in my heart -- tormented me. It drove me to look for love in all the wrong places. Woman after woman, I felt like I was chasing after the wind, unable to catch what I was looking for. All the money or women in the world could not satisfy at all!

In life, men are often tempted by the three "G's:" greed, glory, and girls. I could not get fully satisfied with women. All earthly pleasures had an expiration date, and then that void would come back ten times stronger. I thought my divorce would give me freedom, and life would magically all get better. But it was all a lie!

THE SEARCH FOR THE PERFECT PARTNER

I was on a search for the perfect partner, just enjoying different women like flavors of ice cream. I thought I needed more women.

Money was not an issue at this time, so I flagrantly spent money on fancy meals, dates, and trying to fill that black hole of loneliness. I wined and dined my way through life, and enjoyed all the earthly pleasures. I believed I was living the high life.

Every night, at the end of the day, as my head hit the pillow, that empty, lonely sense of dissatisfaction filled my soul like an unwanted shadow over me. No matter where I ran, I felt lost. No matter how much I tried to fill that void, I knew I was missing something in my life. I just did not know what, or rather *Who* that was. Months passed, but the void grew. God had to help me hit rock bottom and get to the end of myself, so He could bring me to my knees.

STILL STRUGGLING AFTER SALVATION

As I just shared in the previous chapters, Seh Ah's death was that incident that caused me to hit rock bottom. She was the seed that gave birth to my salvation. The very day of her burial was my spiritual birthday. However, as a baby Christian, most of what church people shared did not make sense to me. I still struggled with temptation and sin.

THE SPIRIT OF TRUTH

The Work of the Holy Spirit

"But now I go away to Him who sent Me, and none of you asks Me, 'Where are You going?' But because I have said these things to you, sorrow has filled your heart. Nevertheless I tell you the truth. It is to your advantage that I go away; for if I do not go away, the Helper will not come to you; but if I depart, I will send Him to you. And when He has come, He will convict the world of sin, and of righteousness, and of judgment: of sin, because they do not believe in Me; of righteousness, because I go to My Father and you see Me no more; of judgment, because the ruler of this world is judged.

"I still have many things to say to you, but you cannot bear them now. However, when He, the Spirit of truth, has come, He will guide you into all truth; for He will not speak on His own authority, but whatever He hears He will speak; and He will tell you things to come. He will glorify Me, for He will take of what is Mine and declare it to you. All things that the Father has are Mine. Therefore I said that He will take of Mine and declare it to you." (John 16:5-15)

I had received the Holy Spirit, but I had no clue how to access the power of God within me. Having the Holy Spirit is like having an all-inclusive admission pass to a theme park but not knowing yet that I could go on any ride, or get anything for free.

CHRIST IN ME - THE HOPE OF GLORY

I had to learn what the Bible means when He promises how the Holy Spirit which raised Jesus from the dead lives in me. *"The Spirit of God, who raised Jesus from the dead, lives in you. And just as God raised Christ Jesus from the dead, he will give life to your mortal bodies by this same*

Spirit living within you." (Romans 8:11) How do I access that in my daily life?

The Holy Spirit gives grace to overcome every temptation. But how do we access the Holy Spirit? I felt like I was stumbling forward in the dark just wanting someone to turn on the lights and rescue me from the sin which was so easily entangling me. I wanted to run the race Jesus set before me but felt like my legs were shackled by my struggles. Help me Jesus! How can I truly change my own nature? Only through the Power of the Holy Spirit!

"This is the Word of the Lord Zerubbabel: 'Not by might nor by power, but by My Spirit,' says the LORD Almighty." (Zechariah 4:6)

BY MY SPIRIT

Salvation happens in a moment, but sanctification and growing into the image of Jesus takes a lifetime. My journey of growing in the grace of God should encourage you that if God could help "little old me", He can help anyone.

Joseph was able to overcome not only sexual sin, but also false accusation.

OVERCOMING FALSE ACCUSATION

One of the hardest things to overcome is being falsely accused. Can you imagine how frustrating it would be for Joseph to pass the test of refusing Potiphar's wife's sexual advances, but then be falsely accused by her? No one would believe Joseph after he was falsely accused by Potiphar's wife. But he still walked in meekness, humility, and purity. This is a great testimony to us today. Sometimes, our greatest weapon in the face of accusation is silence.

Jesus stood silent before His accusers. *"He was oppressed and af-flicted, yet he did not open his mouth; he was led like a lamb to the slaughter, and as a sheep before its shearers is silent, so he did not open his mouth."* (Isaiah 53:7)

Here is the best piece on overcoming false accusation by Nolan Clark:

I used to hate being falsely accused. I mean I'd write a book like Au-gustine's Confessions of my real faults, but I've always hated being falsely represented by adversaries.

Then I realized the incredible opportunity it provides to be deeply Christ-like. It's almost the blackbelt of spirituality to be able to play the scapegoat and forgive your slanderers.

I'm not saying I've perfected this, nor do I seek more opportunities to perfect it, but I do love the freedom I feel, and the friendship with the Divine scapegoat it brings.

Love your enemies, forgive your slanderers, and bless those who curse you. Pray that Christ liberates them from the true Adversary who animates their animosity.

Your greatest victory would be to see your enemies liberated not decimated. In this battle you can't be a victorious lion without being a forgiving lamb.

Choose love. Aim your stone at the Giant behind the giant, the Adversary behind the adversary.

"You'll know them by the obvious fruit of their lives and ministries."

Chapter 6
If You Confess Your Sins, He is Faithful

The Bible promises that *"If you confess your sins, He is faithful and right-eous to forgive us of our sins."* (1 John 1:9) We need to confess our sins to God, but we also need to confess our sins one to another to walk in true freedom in Christ. *"Confess your sins one to another and pray for one another that you may be healed. The effective, fervent prayer of a righteous man avails much."* (James 5:16)

God forgives us. We need one another to walk continuously in freedom. It is so sad -- the lost art of vulnerability and accounta-bility in the body of Christ. Once the dust from the funeral settled and I had radically given my life to Jesus, I still did not understand the magnitude of what happened!

I confessed with my mouth that Jesus Christ was now the Lord of my life and had invited Him into my heart, but I was still just an earthenware jar of clay. *"If you declare with your mouth, "Jesus is Lord," and believe in your heart that God raised him from the dead, you will be saved. For it is with your heart that you believe and are justified, and it is with your mouth that you profess your faith and are saved."* (Romans 10:9-10)

For most of us, we are not set free and delivered in a moment. It is not an instant, spontaneous deliverance. In my journey, God humbled me to help me realize how much I need Him but also how much I need my brothers and sisters in the Body of Christ. So after I was saved, I relapsed back into all my sin: lying, women, and growing marijuana. As a new Christian, I did not understand the process of sanctification. I did not understand the concept of 'the old man has passed away and now I am a new creation in Christ' (2 Cor. 5:17). What on earth does this mean? Christians can sometimes sound like they're speaking a foreign language all their own ('Christianese', if you will). So when people told me "my house was cleaned out," it was all Greek to me.

SEVEN TIMES WORSE

"When a corrupting spirit is expelled from someone, it drifts along through the desert looking for an oasis, some unsuspecting soul it can bedevil. When it doesn't find anyone, it says, 'I'll go back to my old haunt.' On return, it finds the person swept and dusted, but vacant. It then runs out and rounds up seven other spirits dirtier than itself and they all move in, whooping it up. That person ends up far worse than if he'd never gotten cleaned up in the first place." (Luke 11:24-26 The Message)

True to this passage, things did not get better, they got worse. I was given over to a reprobate mind. (Romans 1:28) The Bible warns us that if we persist in sin, the demonic spirit comes back with seven others. I had so much trouble fleeing sin. How could I ever get free?

SHALOM IS THE DESTROYER OF CHAOS

The enemy was lying to me and tempting me. Satan was trying to convince me to keep growing pot for five more years, save all the money, and then I could retire once and for all. He was whispering lies in my ears to just work now, so I could enjoy the rest of my life! Sin just a little longer, and no one will know. Grind now, and then vacation later and never have to work again. I was driven to live for tomorrow, but I had no peace in the present. I had no peace in my life.

Shalom in Hebrew means *the destroyer of chaos*. My mind was in chaos and torment. I would weep because I did not understand what was happening to me, and I wanted to stop but really did not know how. I hid my sin in shame, afraid to tell a soul. I lived a double life. I teetered with one foot in the world and one foot in the Church. I love Psalms 34:5-7: *"I sought the LORD, and he answered me; he delivered me from all my fears. Those who look to him are radiant; their faces are never covered with shame…The angel of the LORD encamps around those who fear him, and he delivers them."* This is a promise of the deliverance I didn't even know was possible at this time in my life.

SALVATION TO SANCTIFICATION
TO TRANSFORMATION

When we are saved, we are set apart for God's purposes. God sets people apart from the world to honor him (John 17:15-18; Romans 12:1-2). People are purified from their sins by the blood of Jesus (Hebrews 9:14). However, sanctification is a process – not an instant moment like the moment we accept Jesus as Our Lord and Savior.

Sanctification is the believer's cleansing or purging from the nature of sin. Through grace, people are saved and reconciled to God. It is by grace that we are saved. It is also by grace we become holy and have the nature of God, and reflect the life of our Lord and Saviour, Jesus Christ. How we need the grace of God in every breath and yes of our lives!

GLORY TO GLORY: TRANSFORMED INTO THE SAME IMAGE

Biblically, sanctification is to be conformed to the image of Christ through the power of the Holy Spirit (Romans 8:29). As we are sanctified, we are transformed. If we behold Jesus, we become like Jesus. *"But we all, with unveiled faces, beholding as in a mirror the glory of the Lord, are being transformed into the same image from glory to glory, just as by the spirit of the Lord."* (2 Corinthians 3:18)

FROM GLORY TO GLORY

I want to be in the image of my Heavenly Father just as Jesus was the exact representation of our Father. Glory to glory sounds grand, doesn't it? But the truth is that the process of walking in the finished work of the cross is a lot of blood, sweat and tears.

How do we grow in the grace of God? We need the living Word of God daily, the power of the Holy Spirit and the fellowship of the saints. Eventually, I was invited to a bible study. I was so busy working that I really did not want to go.

But over time, I relented to my friends' insistent invitations and, reluctantly, I went. Like a magnet, something or Someone was drawing me to go each week. This was the first time in my life I had ever heard people teach the Bible in a practical way and how to apply it in your life. Like a baby drinking fresh milk to survive, I listened to every word and hung on for dear life.

TRUE ROCK BOTTOM: ARRESTED AND EXPOSED

When I was arrested, my kingdom came crashing down. Could you imagine if your secret sin became the headline of the local newspapers? In heaven, even our thoughts are laid bare before God. Every secret sin I had done in darkness was being exposed in the light. At the time, how that hurt! But it was really God's kindness which led me to true godly repentance.

I was only a three-month-old baby believer. I was crying out to God day after day. I wanted to be done with this lifestyle, but I did not know how to just come home to The Father.

GOD LOVES ME TOO MUCH TO LEAVE ME TO MYSELF

The Father loves me so much He would not leave me like this. God was gradually cleaning me up. Eight months later, unbeknownst to me, I met my future wife, Elaine. This only fueled a desire in me to live a godly life and lead as a patriarch. I tried to remember that whenever I was looking at a woman, if I wanted to be treated as royalty, I must take care of the king's daughter. I wanted, no matter how much I struggled, to honor Elaine. We would do our best to strive to walk in holiness as we were dating. We dated for two years, then got married.

RESTORING THE FOUNDATIONS

After my jail cell, I tried my hardest to follow Him, to read my bible, and to learn how to apply it to my life. I was learning how to hear His voice. The Father was faithfully transforming me, though sometimes it was one step forward and two steps backwards. The Father knew that I did not have total freedom from sexual addiction even though I thought I had conquered it once and for all.

A number of years after my wife and I got married, He was directing me to sign up for a ministry called Restoring the Foundations (RTF). RTF defines itself: *The core revelation of all Restoring the Foundations personal ministry and all our ministry training is the Integrated Approach to Biblical Healing. This is bedrock. The revelation is that there are four sources of all of our problems and they are integrally intertwined. There is an inter-relatedness among Generational Sins and Curses which we inherit and which pressure us to follow the same patterns as our ancestors; Ungodly Beliefs, or lies that we believe; Soul/Spirit Hurts which are hurts and wounds from life; and Demonic Oppression that keeps us stuck in the negative patterns. In order to bring lasting healing and freedom, we minister to all four sources of the problems during the time of ministry.*

At first, I thought I was fine. After all, my life had changed. I was not dealing drugs or living the way I was before. I was truly a new man, or so I thought! But He was nudging me to go get a spiritual 'house cleaning'. I listened and my wife and I both signed up to work on ourselves, our marriage and laying a godly foundation in our family.

ENCOUNTER DURING RTF

Restoring The Foundations is a week-long intensive where there are two trained facilitators for each person. It's a 5-to-6 day session, each session about 3 to 4 hours per person, they also have intercessors that are praying before and during the sessions. Though it's really the Holy Spirit that is doing the work, not the facilitators. It is like a week-long heart surgery. It changed my life and was a turning point.

During the one-week healing and deliverance ministry, there was something dramatic that happened to me one particular day. As we were breaking off and confessing all the ungodly soul ties and asking for forgiveness (and forgiving myself), I suddenly got very nauseous! I thought I was going to pass out and fall flat on the floor. I fought to keep my composure and not collapse.

The Holy Spirit is faithful to heal us. At the end of the session, the facilitator said that I looked like I was about to fall over. I explained to her what I felt and she responded with the prophetic vision she saw as they ministered to me.

DELIVERED OF A SLIME SUIT OF DEMONIC LUST

In the spirit, the facilitator saw a slime suit covering my entire body like a onesie that a young child would wear. She saw the slime suit come right off and fly out the window. In the Scripture, Jesus clearly commands us to cast out demons. For example, in Matthew 10:7-8: *"As you go, proclaim this message: 'The kingdom of heaven has come near. Heal the sick, raise the dead, cleanse lepers, cast out demons. You have received without paying, give without pay."*

If Jesus' disciples who were taught by the Ultimate Rabbi – Jesus – were commanded to cast out demons, how much more should we follow in their footsteps? Jesus commanded us in Mark 16:17: *"And these signs will accompany those who believe: in my name, they will cast out demons; they will speak in new tongues."* We are commanded to cast out demons as a sign of following Jesus!

WASHED WHITER THAN SNOW

Psalms 51:1-7
"Have mercy upon me, O God,
According to Your lovingkindness;
According to the multitude of Your tender mercies,
Blot out my transgressions.
Wash me thoroughly from my iniquity,
And cleanse me from my sin.
For I acknowledge my transgressions,
And my sin is always before me.
Against You, You only, have I sinned,
And done this evil in Your sight—
That You may be found just when You speak,
And blameless when You judge.
Behold, I was brought forth in iniquity,
And in sin my mother conceived me.
Behold, You desire truth in the inward parts,
And in the hidden part You will make me to know wisdom.
Purge me with hyssop, and I shall be clean;
Wash me, and I shall be whiter than snow."

That day, I randomly chose to wear a white shirt that I had never worn before! The Holy Spirit spoke to the facilitator and said,

"Look at the white shirt Mark is wearing. He's pure now and whiter than snow!"

HE DELIVERED ME BECAUSE HE DELIGHTS IN ME

Almost how the Seraphim came to Isaiah in Chapter 6 to purify him, impart holiness, and commission him in this divine encounter, I was instantly delivered from lust. My life was forever changed. I had spent my entire life struggling and now was pure. Psalms 18:19 promises: *"He also brought me out into a broad place; He delivered me because He delighted in me."*

One of my favorite life verses is 2 Timothy 2:21: *"Those who cleanse themselves from the latter will be instruments for special purposes, made holy, useful to the Master and prepared to do any good work."* When we yield to the pain of the process of sanctification, we come forth as gold and are set apart as an instrument for Him. I am closing this chapter with one of the best embodiments of sanctification – the metaphor of the pearl. We are Jesus' pearl of great price:

PEARLS OF PURITY

Did you know that an oyster that has not been wounded in any way does not produce pearls? A pearl is a healed wound.

Pearls are a product of pain. The result of a foreign or unwanted substance (such as a parasite or grain of sand) entering the oyster.

The inside of an oyster shell is a shiny substance called "nacre." When a grain of sand enters, the nacre cells go to work and cover that sand with layers and more layers to protect the defenseless body of the oyster. As a result, a beautiful pearl is formed! The more pearls, the more valuable. Maybe when you first see the purity and beauty of a pearl, you would not imagine that it is only formed and fashioned from the pain of the process - just like our own lives in God.

God never allows pain without a purpose.

What if your greatest ministry to others comes out of your greatest hurt or deepest wounds? Nothing compares to the glory that will be revealed in us (Romans 8:17-18).

Elaine and I at Stanley Park the day we got married.

Chapter 7
Living Loved

Never forget that our dreams must first come from a place where our identity is secure in God's unconditional love for us.

Joseph bragged about his dreams as his identity was in his dreams. In this passage of Genesis 37-50, we see how Joseph's brothers mocked and ridiculed Joseph. Can any of you relate to being tested by your prophetic promise? There will always be those who laugh at you and say, "Here comes the dreamer!"

Joseph's dreams got him ridiculed, betrayed, and eventually thrown into a waterless pit. His journey from waterless pit to a palace took over fourteen years. He missed fourteen years of his life with his beloved father Jacob (whom he was Jacob's favorite!) He was not mature and God used the process of pruning to mature him.

DREAMING CAN BE DANGEROUS

Dreaming can be dangerous, as Joseph learned the hard way. With his youthful zeal and pride, he blurted out his dreams to his brothers, provoking them to jealousy. Sometimes those who are called to celebrate us most betray us out of their jealousy. Unfortunately,

I have made the same mistake Joseph did at the beginning of my journey where I would excitedly share the prophetic words over my life. My wife was actually secretly praying that I would stop. Thank you, Jesus, for the power of praying wives! The Holy Spirit convicted me to stop and to hide some promises and ponder them in my heart the way Mary did in Luke 1. Identity must first be rooted in God, not in the Earth assignments He gives us to do.

We must be so secure in God's opinion of us, and live before the Audience of One. If you do not know God's value for you and purpose for your life, someone else will give you his or her purpose. Purposes must first be rooted in identity. Doing must flow from being. We are human beings – not human doings.

ONENESS IN CHRIST

"...that all of them may be one, Father, just as you are in me and I am in you. May they also be in us so that the world may believe that you have sent me. I have given them the glory that you gave me, that they may be one as we are one--I in them and you in me--so that they may be brought to complete unity. Then the world will know that you sent me and have loved them even as you have loved me." (John 17:21- 23)

What does it mean to have our identity in God? How do we live the way Jesus prayed we would in John 17? He prayed this in the garden of Gethsemane, just before he went to the cross. How do we live in oneness with Father, Son and Holy Spirit? It has taken me a lifetime to learn to "live loved." To live from the place of realizing that "the joy set before Him" was me. (Hebrews 12:2)

I am His inheritance. He is my reward. Jesus really is the dream. All our callings must flow from intimacy. All fruitfulness flows from abiding.

LOOKING UNTO JESUS

How do we live looking unto Jesus, the Author and Finisher of our faith, rather than comparing ourselves to others? (Hebrews 12:2) If Joseph had looked to his brothers, he would have been depressed when he found himself in a waterless pit, then Potiphar's house, and finally prison. How did Joseph look to the Author and Finisher of his faith even in prison?

PROPHET IN TRAINING = P.I.T.

"It is better to risk starving to death than surrender. If you give up on your dreams, what's left?" -- Jim Carrey

Have you ever doubted God's promises when they take years or even decades to come to pass? Has your heart ever grown faint from waiting? Proverbs 13:12 warns us that *"hope deferred makes the heart sick, but a longing fulfilled is a tree of life."*

It took fourteen years from the pit to the prison to the palace! Graham Cooke, an established prophet, also said it was a fourteen-year journey for a prophet to be formed. Sometimes, we find ourselves in a pit on our way to our destiny, and we simply give up faith.

IT TAKES FAITH TO PLEASE GOD

Sometimes in the process of being established in your calling, you can feel like you have fallen off the roadmap of your divine destiny. But without faith, it is impossible to please God! Hebrews 11:6 promises: *"And without faith it is impossible to please God because anyone who comes to him must believe that He exists and that He rewards those who earnestly seek Him.*"

In this "momentary lightness of affliction," we can give The Father the gift of our trust (2 Cor. 4:17- 18). Can you imagine if Joseph's identity was dependent on external success? He would have been depressed for years! He would have thought that God had abandoned him, and that his dreams as a young boy were false!

Remember how God promises in 1 Samuel 16:7: *"Do not consider his appearance or his height, for I have rejected him. The LORD does not look at the things people look at. People look at the outward appearance, but the LORD looks at the heart."* What would it look like if we calibrated our life's success in terms of loving God and loving others – rather than the measures of earthly success?

THE WORD OF THE LORD TESTED JOSEPH

In the dark dingy prison cell, the word of the Lord tested Joseph. During this challenging season, I believe Joseph forged such deep fellowship with The Father in the fiery furnace of affliction. Joseph knew he could not make his dreams come true in his own strength. So he learned to live from rest.

LEARNING TO LIVE FROM REST

On June 22, 2019, I had a prophetic dream which was an invitation from the Father, like Joseph, to learn to live from rest.

In the dream, I was surrounded by the racquetball courts that I usually play on. I peered through the glass courts, but there were no players at the popular sports club I frequented. The scene shifted: The whole court was set up like a beautifully organized living room with couches and chairs. The second court also transformed into a living room. And then, the third court became a living room as well. What was The Father saying in the puzzle pieces of my dream? The Father was inviting me into His rest. It was time to stop running around like a hamster on a wheel striving and sweating. I tried to earn acceptance through my own works. Instead, the Father asked me to take my place as a beloved son in the living room of communion and union with Him. The Father sweetly invited me into a place of His rest.

BOB JONES'S 100 YEAR PROPHECY

Bob Jones, one of the founding fathers in the prophetic movement in America, was caught up in a visitation where the Father showed him the decades before Jesus' return. The decade 2020 would be marked by a decade of His rest.

"The 2020s will reveal the rest of God. To where the body will come into a place of resting in God, where God will rest in us. And in this rest, the enemy will not be able to do warfare because we are resting in God and He is resting in us, and He will accomplish the things He means to do in a people that is at rest. He has always wanted a people that will come into His rest. There never has been one but rest is on the way."

THE ENEMY HAS NO HOLD OVER ME

I can honestly and truthfully say that the devil has no legal right over me anymore. In John 14:30, Jesus said, *"I will not say much more to you, for the prince of this world is coming, but he has no hold on me."*

Just like Jesus said that the devil had nothing he could accuse Jesus of, I believe we can learn to walk in such integrity that there is no way for the devil to influence us in our lives. In a nutshell, being in His rest means dying to your own works completely – so now God can work in you, with you, and through you. You are now full of God and not full of yourself. You are now possessed by God - the temple that He dwells in.

Joseph had to learn to enter into His rest. I think he got to the end of himself where God became His dream.

SITTING AT THE TABLE OF THE LORD

"He is more eager to answer than we are to ask." ~Smith Wigglesworth

The Lord also gave me multiple dreams about how He prepares a feast for us and a place at the table that only His people can fill. The Father did not want me to only feast off listening to well-respected teachers in the Body of Christ anymore. He wanted to feed me directly from His own hands. He was instructing me personally not to eat leftovers from the plates of others. I have had many dreams about Him feeding me directly, as we are in the kitchen together. He is preparing a feast for His people. He is the Bread of Life.

HOW TO BE WITH JESUS

The Bible is the only Living Word. Sometimes, it is overwhelming to learn how to spend time with God. But The Father wants to meet with us more than we want to meet with Him. You might only have time for one chapter a day. Read for depth and not breadth.

MIKE BICKLE'S FREE TEACHINGS

As I was reading more and more of the Bible, I loved going line by line through the Sermon on the Mount and even taught it in a small group. A great teaching on the Sermon of the Mount is from Mike Bickle, founder of the International House of Prayer in Kansas City, Missouri. He is, in my opinion, one of the greatest teachers in the body of Christ (and all of his teachings can be found free online). As I went through this verse-by-verse study, the Father took me through the 'seminary of hard knocks' to really learn how to live loved and to live the Beatitudes as my own lifestyle. When you read the Scriptures, it is so important to apply this to your life! It is not about head knowledge, you want "heart" or revelation knowledge.

AT HIS FEET

I like to set the first two to three hours of my day just being at His feet. I try to get to bed by 10:30 at night so I can wake up at dawn with Your song.

"Arise, my soul, and sing his praises! I will awaken the dawn with my worship, greeting the daybreak with my songs of light." (Psalm 108:2)

My quiet times are just that. I usually will get up between 3am and 5am before the sun even rises and before anyone else is awake. The night is quiet. No one can compete for your time and attention.

TALK TO HIM LIKE A FRIEND

Some of us feel like when we talk to Jesus, our words bounce off the ceiling and go nowhere. When you have a best friend, you usually communicate with them frequently. You do not need to speak in hymns or formalities. Speak to Jesus as if He is your best friend.

LIVE LOVED

Learning to live from rest, abiding in Him and living loved is key. We need to learn to feast on Him alone. I want to end with one of my favorite passages about entering rest.

HEBREWS 4:1-13:
THE FAITH REST LIFE (TPT)

Now the promise of entering into God's rest is still for us today. So we must be extremely careful to ensure that we all embrace the fullness of that promise and not fail to experience it. For we have heard the good news of deliverance just as they did, yet they didn't join their faith with the Word. Instead, what they heard didn't affect them deeply, for they doubted. For those of us who believe, faith activates the promise and we experience the realm of confident rest! For he has said, 'I was grieved with them and made a solemn oath, 'They will not enter into my rest.' '' God's works have all been completed from the foundation of the world, for it says in the Scriptures, And on the seventh day God rested from all his works. And again, as stated before, They will not enter into my rest. Those who first heard the good news of deliverance failed to enter into that realm of faith's rest because of their unbelieving hearts. Yet the fact remains that we still have the opportunity to enter into the faith-rest life and experience the fulfillment of the promise! For God still has ordained a day for us to enter into called "Today." For it was long afterwards that God repeated it in David's words, "If only today you would listen to his voice and do not harden your hearts!" Now if this promise of "rest" was fulfilled when Joshua brought the people into the land, God wouldn't have spoken later of another "rest" yet to come. So we conclude that there is still a full and complete Sabbath-rest waiting for believers to experience. As we enter into God's faith-rest life we cease from our own works, just as God celebrates his finished works and rests in them. So then we must be eager to experience this faith-rest life, so that no one falls short by following the same pattern of doubt and unbelief. For we have the living Word of God, which is full of energy, like a two-mouthed sword. It will even penetrate to the very core of our being where soul and spirit, bone and marrow meet! It interprets and reveals the true thoughts and secret motives of our hearts. There is not one person who can hide their thoughts from God, for nothing that we do remains a secret, and nothing created is concealed, but everything is exposed and defenseless before his eyes, to whom we must render an account."

"I have called you out of darkness and into the light.
So now go and love one another."
(Elaine Danalis' painting, courtesy of Cinnamon Cooney, the art Sherpa)

Chapter 8
You Cannot Kill A God
Dream

"Remember to celebrate milestones as you prepare for the road ahead." -- Nelson Mandela. The only person who can stop you from your divine destiny is you. Our enemies may plot against us, but God can work all things *"together for the good for those who love Him..."* (Romans 8:28). The journey of Joseph reveals how God's storyline in our lives is so sovereign. Joseph's dreams as a boy eventually came to pass – just years and even decades later.

When Joseph was a boy adorned in his coat of many colors, he was the favorite of his father Jacob. God gave him two dreams which provoked Joseph's brothers to jealousy. They sold him into slavery and Joseph eventually went into prison. But God redeemed this gift and gave Joseph an ability to interpret dreams. It was also his God-given ability to interpret dreams that released him from prison and into the palace which we will discuss in the chapter ahead. Joseph's character, gifting and charisma followed him to prison as well, and the warden soon appointed him as his right-hand man.

TWO DREAMS: CUPBEARER AND BAKER

In time, his unique gifts from the Holy Spirit again manifested: when the king's royal cupbearer and baker were imprisoned, Joseph successfully interpreted their dreams, correctly predicting that the cupbearer would be released and the baker hanged.

Since I was saved, I have been a dreamer. It is one of the main ways that God speaks to me. I will include some of my dreams in the chapters ahead. Joel 2 and Acts 2:17 prophesies how on the last day even "old men shall dream dreams." Now, I am older, but the Father has spoken directly to me through my dreams since I was saved at the age of forty-six.

Joseph had been in prison for months. When the cupbearer was promoted, Joseph asked him to remember him and tell Pharaoh who he was in the hopes of being released.

LOOK TO JESUS--NOT MAN--TO DELIVER YOU

Hebraic Scholars believe Joseph stayed in prison for two more years because Joseph looked to the cupbearer to deliver him and for his salvation instead of trusting the Lord. Sometimes our walk with God feels like one step forward and two steps back. We must always keep our eyes locked on Jesus and trust in God alone – rather than looking to man. We always want to wait on God for our Isaac - sons of promise – rather than make an Ishmael happen in our own strength.

THE WORD OF THE LORD TESTING JOSEPH

"Don't give up on your dreams, or your dreams will give up on you." -- John Wooden

Psalm 105:19 says: *"Until the time that His word came to pass, the word of the Lord tested him."* The word of the Lord tested Joseph.

What does that look like? God had spoken a better word over Joseph than his challenging circumstances, but it must have been difficult for Joseph not to doubt in the word of the Lord. Have you ever doubted that your own prophetic words would come to pass? Have you ever been disappointed in how God fulfills His promises in His timing and not your own? I have struggled in my own journey. For example, I remember before I was imprisoned overnight, a friend had prophesied over me about how she saw greatness in my future. I remember lying on the bed in the jail cell and remembering those words. *How could God ever use me? How could greatness come from this mess of my life?* I thought maybe my one claim to fame would be my cameo appearance on Channel 22 reporting the drug bust! Maybe my best days were behind me. The enemy was whispering in my ears that I had disqualified myself from the call of God! How could the Father ever use "little ole me?" But God is rich in mercy.

DO NOT COMPARE OR COMPETE

The enemy often lays the trap of competition and comparison. Joseph could not compare himself to the cupbearer when he was released two years prior. We cannot compare, compete, or judge externally. We need to focus on staying in our own lane.

FAILING FORWARD

"The only thing worse than starting something and failing... is not starting something." -- Seth Godin.

We have to keep trying and realizing that risk is part of the process. Growing in God means failing forward. Part of maturity is just simply trying. In Proverbs 24:16 we read: *"For though a righteous man falls seven times, they rise again, but the wicked stumble when calamity strikes."* It is not about if you fall down. Even a righteous man stumbles. We all fall short of God's glory. The measure of a man is about repenting, getting yourself back up and into the game.

The day the federal court case was settled in January, 2009, I walked out the door, side by side with Vinny, shook his hand, and smiled. But it was nothing compared to the first time I walked out of jail on April 12th, 2008. That day, I felt the sunshine warmly smile into the very core of my spirit, as if the Father Himself was exonerating me. After spending tens of thousands of dollars on legal bills, I walked out a free man. I had paid my debt in full. I had fallen, but I rose again. Jesus had paid my debt in every way. How amazing is God's grace!

THE GLORY OF BEING TRANSFORMED IN THE MONOTONY OF THE MUNDANE

A year after everything was legally settled in court, my sister-in-law encouraged me to seek the Lord, fast, pray and ask the Lord for His word over my life. What was my purpose? What was my destiny? So, I fasted for two and a half days simply seeking the face of God. The following Sunday at church, a well-respected global prophet named Dennis Cramer gave me an incredible word about the calling on my life. Dennis went one-by-one with a tape recorder and gave many people a word. He encouraged me not to throw out the word the Lord had given me, even if it took time to come to pass.

A friend transcribed the prophetic word so I could pray it into being. I would read and reread the word about my future and life, just as Paul instructed Timothy, *"I am giving you this command in keeping with the prophecies once made about you, so that by recalling them you may fight the battle well"* (1 Timothy 1:18). This is how we wage war with our prophecies, by recalling them and reminding ourselves of God's promises…. But then reality called, work awaited me, and I had to fold up the paper, put it into my dusty desk drawer, and go to work, all while waiting for that word to come to pass. There is a glory about being transformed in the monotony of the mundane and the holiness of hiddenness. I had a choice: I could look at my outward circumstances and shrink back in despair. Or, I could remind God of who He is and what He has said over my life. Sometimes we have to do what Paul commanded Timothy to do.

I had a choice: I could look at my outward circumstances and shrink back in despair. Or, I could remind God of who He is and what He has said over my life.

DO NOT RUSH, BUT TRUST THE PROCESS

In my journey, I have learned to embrace the gift of hiddenness. God hides us to prepare us for our calling. Jesus was prepared for thirty years as the perfect Son before He was the ultimate Savior. Moses waited forty years. Daniel was eighty years old when he received his first prophetic dream. David was 30 when he became king of Israel, approximately 15 years after Samuel anointed him. I was saved at 46 years old, but God hid me for years in my restaurant business which was my crucible of the refiner's fire (more on this later). If we rush the process, we can fall prey to self-promotion. If we try to self-promote and open doors in our own strength, gifting, charisma or efforts -- rather than allowing the Father to open them -- we also have to keep those doors open in our own strength. That is exhausting! We cannot despise the day of small beginnings.

It is better to trust the process and yield to Jesus' perfect leadership over our lives. We cannot make our prophetic words come to pass. Joseph could not make the words over his own life happen. The goal is to dream such God-sized dreams that it requires all of heaven to fulfill the Word of the Lord.

PHAROAH'S TWO DREAMS

Two years later, Joseph was brought before his greatest test. King Pharaoh himself had two dreams, which none of his advisors were able to explain. Recalling the Hebrew youth from his prison days, the cupbearer finally remembered Joseph! The cupbearer suggested that Joseph be summoned.

Joseph, then thirty, interpreted Pharaoh's dreams as being a divine prediction for seven years of plenty followed by seven years of famine. After interpreting this warning from the Lord, Joseph advised Pharaoh to prepare by storing grain during the first seven years, so that there would be food during the famine.

Impressed by Joseph's wisdom and revelation, Pharaoh appointed him as his viceroy, second only to the king himself, and tasked Joseph with readying the nation for the years of famine. Pharaoh recognized Joseph's God-given ability! Pharaoh promoted him to the chief administrator of Egypt. When the favor of

God is in your life, promotion will follow you. No one and nothing can stop you but you!

Leadership is a mantle that we grow in. Just like David was tested with the lion, the bear, and then Goliath, we have seasons to mature us which is our seminary in the spirit. Trials are oftentimes our training for reigning.

VISION OF GOD PROMOTING ME

Clean Garments for the High Priest

Then he showed me Joshua the high priest standing before the angel of the LORD, and Satan standing at his right side to accuse him. The LORD said to Satan, "The LORD rebuke you, Satan! The LORD, who has chosen Jerusalem, rebuke you! Is not this man a burning stick snatched from the fire?" Now Joshua was dressed in filthy clothes as he stood before the angel. The angel said to those who were standing before him, "Take off his filthy clothes." Then he said to Joshua, "See, I have taken away your sin, and I will put fine garments on you. (Zechariah 3:1-5)

During this season of waiting for the Lords promises, God gave me a profound dream. In my dream, the Lord instructed me to put my head to the ground, and keep working hard in humility. The Father told me to wait as He was behind closed doors rebuking the enemy in my life. Just like Zechariah 3:1-5, Satan stands before The Father night and day and accuses us.

Even though I, like Joshua, was guilty of sin, The Father was working behind the scenes, defeating the enemy who sought to destroy my destiny. The Father drew a line in the sand. Because of the power of His blood, He speaks a better word over my iniquity. I heard the Father say in my dream, "I got you a job, promotion and advancement!" The Father promised to promote me Himself.

God is the one who makes us fruitful. We are simply called to be faithful.

NAME CHANGE

The Pharaoh renamed Joseph "Zaphenath - Paneah" which translates to "Revealer of the Dream." Joseph had such a supernatural gift to interpret dreams through the spirit of wisdom and revelation (Eph. 1:17) that it marked his life. His reputation went before him. Like Joseph, I love revelation. I enjoy studying the Hebrew meaning in words to dig deeper in revelation. Let's examine the Hebrew letter "Nun."

NUN: HEBREW LETTER FOR SEED OR FISH

The fourteenth letter of the Hebrew aleph-bet is a picture of a seed or a fish perpetuating and propagating, as in from one generation to another. Hebrew letters have pictorial and numerical significance. The Hebrew letter of "Nun" also correlates with the number "50."

Prophetic words are seeds like this Hebrew letter "Nun." We have to water them with faith. As we add our faith to His word, it births the prophetic word into fruition. The Bible promises that, *"Without faith, it is impossible to please God."* (Hebrews 11:6)

THE WORD ACCOMPLISHES HIS WILL

"For as the rain and snow come down from heaven, And do not return there without watering the earth, Making it bear and sprout, And providing seed to

the sower and bread to the eater. So will My word be which goes out in My mouth; It will not return to Me void (useless, without result), Without accomplishing what I desire, And without succeeding in the matter for which I sent it." (Isaiah 55:10-11)

What if we really believed that God's Word would not return to Him void? What if we believed that the Bible was living and active - sharper than a two-edged sword? That with every prophetic word also comes the empowering grace to fulfill it?

There is a pandemic in the Western Church of prayerlessness and biblical illiteracy. The Bride of Christ must wake up!

WAKE UP, SLEEPING BEAUTY, WAKE UP!

We must watch our words. Words create worlds. God spoke, and the Universe was formed. I believe that when Joseph was in the dungeon, he was pacing back and forth reminding God of His promises. During my three years of probation, I clung to my prophetic promises for dear life. I had to make a deliberate choice to live by faith rather than by sight. I had to cultivate an attitude of gratitude no matter how my circumstances looked.

The Israelites would always build altars of remembrance to remind themselves of God's faithfulness. Sometimes we can take our prophecies and wage war with them. Quoting the written Word of God and praying for our prophetic promises in our lives will literally shift our destiny.

THE NUMBER "50"

The Hebrew letter "Nun" is multifaceted. It correlates with the number "50," which symbolizes jubilee and the supernatural. In

Hebrew culture, the Book of Leviticus commands us to take off every 50th year as part of the law given by Yahweh to the Israelites. Every 50 years, all debt was forgiven, land was returned to its rightful owners, the land rested from labor, and all the slaves were set free. I believe we are to live from rest.

Nun also means a "servant" or a soul. One lesson I have learned in my own life is that the key to greatness is to become the servant of all. In the chapter ahead, I will be sharing my journey serving in the restaurant business.

THE GREATEST IS THE SERVANT OF ALL

"But he who is greatest among you shall be your servant. And for those who exalt themselves will be humbled and those who humble themselves will be exalted." (Matthew 23:11-12)

Why is it so important to become the servant of all? *"God opposes the proud and gives grace to the humble."* (James 4:6) Dr. Heidi Baker always preaches how, *"the River of God rushes to the lowest place. So go 'low and slow' because it attracts God."* The Father cannot resist humility. Jesus was meek and lowly of heart.

THE HUMBLED AND EXALTED CHRIST

Let this mind be in you which was also in Christ Jesus, who, being in the form of God, did not consider it robbery to be equal with God, but made Himself of no reputation, taking the form of a bondservant, and coming in the likeness of men. And being found in the appearance as a man, He humbled Himself and became obedient to the point of death, even the death of the cross. Therefore God also has highly exalted Him and given Him the name which is above every name, that at the name of Jesus every knee should bow, of those in heaven, and of those on earth, and of those under the earth, and that every tongue should confess that Jesus Christ is Lord, to the glory of God the Father. (Philippians 2:5-11)

Jesus is our model for ministry. He made Himself of no reputation. The door of humility is the key for apostolic leadership. Another great example of this is in the life of Moses. *"Now the man Moses was very meek, above all the men which were upon the face of the earth."* (Num. 12:3) Moses was described as the humblest man of all, but he also moved in unprecedented signs and wonders! Both in the example of Jesus and Moses, God calls us to be the servant of all.

When we lay down our lives for one another, it attracts the supernatural. Oftentimes, God brings miracles at 11:59 pm -- the last moment when we are desperate for a breakthrough. When we depend on ourselves, we do not need the supernatural. "Nun" -- or our need attracts God.

It was when Moses, standing on the edge of the Red Sea -- facing the impossibility of the fierce, incoming Egyptian army -- that Israel had a great need for deliverance! Moses watched in awe as God parted the Red Sea and swept away the enemies of Israel. When we come to God as humble servants, our humility causes us to be fully dependent on God. When we become completely aware of our absolute need for Him and dependent like a child, we attract the supernatural.

Provision pursues humility. Signs follow the Word. Humility attracts the supernatural. The Bible promises in the Beatitudes, *"Blessed are the meek, for they shall inherit the earth"* (Matthew 5:5). We are called to *"take the nations as our inheritance and the ends of the earth as our possession"* (Psalms 2:8). We have to be meek to be conquerors in the kingdom of God. We must dream big with God!

DARE TO DREAM: DO IT SCARED

"COURAGE doesn't mean we are never scared. Courage is ACTION in the face of fear." Ruth Soukup

The enemy will even try to steal, or kill your dreams, but we cannot quit dreaming! To not dream is even more dangerous. In fact, it is death. Dare to dream. Do not let fear rob you. Fear is faith in the enemy. It is the opposite of love. We must live life fearlessly. Sometimes we need to do things even when we are scared.

MOTHER TERESA'S "ANYWAY" POEM

People are often unreasonable, illogical and self centered;
Forgive them anyway.
If you are kind, people may accuse you of selfish, ulterior motives;
Be kind anyway.
If you are successful, you will win some false friends and some true enemies;
Succeed anyway.
If you are honest and frank, people may cheat you;
Be honest and frank anyway.
What you spend years building, someone could destroy overnight;
Build anyway.
If you find serenity and happiness, they may be jealous;
Be happy anyway.
The good you do today, people will often forget tomorrow;
Do good anyway.
Give the world the best you have, and it may never be enough;
Give the world the best you've got anyway.

You see, in the final analysis, it is between you and your God;
It was never between you and them anyways.

"Seven years of great abundance are coming throughout the land of Egypt, but seven years of famine will follow them."

Chapter 9
Promotion Comes
from The Lord:
Double Fruitfulness

TOMMASO'S RESTAURANT

When you imagine the movie, "My Big, Fat Greek Wedding," you might picture a Greek family bustling around a table like New York Times Square, spraying Windex, feasting, talking over each other and shouting, "Opa!" My life wasn't too far off; through high school, food was always a part of our Greek culture and family. I have so many fun childhood memories gathering around a Greek Feast at a family meal.

Naturally, God led me into the restaurant industry as I always had a heart for creating family memories around food. Before I was saved, I spent almost thirty years in either the restaurant or real estate business. In 1980, after I graduated high school, I went to Rhode Island School of Design and studied two years of culinary arts. After I graduated in 1982, I started working in the restaurant

GOD MEANT IT FOR GOOD

industry. Sometimes I would pull long hours from 7am to 11pm at Tilly's Restaurant - a very fast paced, hopping business. I love people so this industry fit me well. I worked such long hours I almost thought I should build a bed in the restaurant.

After we had struck a deal to pay the government $650,000, the authorities no longer viewed me as a threat. I was able to buy my own restaurant – Tommaso's. I was working amicably to make all my past mistakes right.

I appreciate the story of Joseph, as he was so hard working which I think is a lost ethic in our modern day world. Joseph had a "King Midas touch" where everything he touched turned to gold. Whether he was promoted in Potiphar's house or prison, his character commanded a blessing. I realized I had a similar grace. When I was growing pot, I had almost a supernatural bumper crop. God taught me through blood, sweat and tears how to work very hard as if I was working for him, and create a business.

THE GREATEST IS THE SERVANT OF ALL WORKING AS UNTO THE LORD

David's first church was worshiping and feeding sheep on the back side of the desert. My first ministry was found in a hot kitchen cooking up a storm with a heart to serve my community. Only God could take a former drug dealer and help him to set up an honorable business in the same town he sold drugs! I happily served in secret and worked hard as unto the Lord. *"Whatever you do, work at it with all your heart, as working for the Lord, not for human masters, since you know that you will receive an inheritance from the Lord as a reward. It is the Lord Christ you are serving."* (Colossians 3:23-24)

The very community I was arrested in, I served with such gratitude as I earned money honorably. I found great joy working hard and quietly. God put Adam in the Garden of Eden to work hard before the fall. So working hard is part of godly character. *"And to make it your ambition to lead a quiet life; you should mind your own business and work with your hands, just as we told you, so that your daily life may win the respect of outsiders and so that you will not be dependent on anybody."* (1 Thes. 4:11-12)

MY RESTAURANT WAS LIKE MY SEMINARY

I owned and led the restaurant for nine years, and God used it like a seminary in the spirit for me. I was the main chef, host, manager, and owner in this fun Italian/American mom and pop shop, which only seated one hundred and eleven people.

Over a short period of time, I realized that the restaurant was actually a ministry. This was my "training for reigning." God did a deep work of character in my life. I had to learn how to trust in God and learn how to collaborate. I went from bringing in large amounts of cash a week from my pot business to earning a normal salary. This was very humbling for me. But God sees us when no one else does. And when we do everything in secret as unto Him, He rewards us openly.

JOSEPH GREW IN FAVOR

The Father enabled Joseph to do things in secret as unto Him. Character attracts favor which precipitates promotion. Joseph found favor with both Pharoah and Potiphar. After appointing Joseph as viceroy, Pharaoh gave him as a wife Asenath, daughter of

Potiphera, priest of On. Joseph refused to sleep with Potiphar's wife. She betrayed him and lied about him. Joseph endured being falsely accused.

MY WIFE ELAINE

Moral Benefits of Wisdom
My son, if you accept my words
and store up my commands within you,
turning your ear to wisdom
and applying your heart to understanding—
indeed, if you call out for insight
and cry aloud for understanding,
and if you look for it as for silver
and search for it as for hidden treasure,
then you will understand the fear of the LORD
and find the knowledge of God.
For the LORD *gives wisdom;*
from his mouth come knowledge and understanding.
He holds success in store for the upright,
he is a shield to those whose walk is blameless,
for he guards the course of the just
and protects the way of his faithful ones.
(Proverbs 2:1-8)

In July 2008, I met my beautiful wife, Elaine. I was only a baby Christian. We met at Panera Bread Restaurant and sat across from each other and shared for hours. I sought the Lord to see if Elaine was the one He chose for me. We started to date and I wanted to know that it was an alignment from heaven. After reading Proverbs 2:1-8, I searched and scoured the Bible on every verse about marriage and how God defines a godly woman. The Lord gave me a dream with a wedding dress…

DREAM ABOUT MARRYING ELAINE

A month later, after working an eighteen-hour shift in the restaurant, I asked the Lord for a sign. Every cell of my body was beyond exhausted. I showered, crawled into bed and opened my Bible. It fell open to Proverbs 3:5-6: *"Trust in the LORD with all your heart and lean not on your own understanding; in all your ways submit to him, and he will make your paths straight."* I needed The Father to help me make my crooked paths straight and know for certain that Elaine was my bride and prize.

For weeks, Elaine and I took a premarital class in our church. The day we were supposed to get the results back from our pastor about our compatibility test, the Lord clearly spoke to me and interpreted the dream for me. The Father said, "Elaine is the one I have given you and you are to marry her now." He said that if I followed Proverbs 3:5-6, He would make our lives and our paths straight together. At that moment, He joyfully confirmed that I should marry Elaine. I walked into our final premarital counseling meeting with a smile on my face. Elaine waited with baited breath for my surprise. She was nervous because she had no idea what I was about to say. I shared the good news of how the Father had faithfully confirmed we were meant to be married. The Pastor sweetly smiled and asked if we wanted to know how we did on the test? We said "Yes". He responded, "You guys are compatible and you are getting married."

PASSED WITH FLYING COLORS

We had passed our test with flying colors. On May 2nd, 2010, Elaine and I got married! She truly is God's highest and best for me and the woman of my dreams. *"If you consent and obey, You will eat the best of the land."* (Isaiah 1:19) God truly writes the best love stories! As a blended family, we had six children altogether.

MANASSEH AND EPHRAIM

Joseph and Asenath had two sons, Manasseh and Ephraim, both born during the seven years of plenty. Indeed, throughout the Jews' journey in the desert, the tribes of Manasseh and Ephraim received equal status to the other tribes, and they inherited individual portions of the Land of Israel after Jacob passed. They were the only ones of Jacob's grandchildren to receive the same inheritance as his own sons.

MEANING OF NAMES

In the Bible, names are so significant. Manasseh translates to, "God has caused me to forget all my troubles." Ephraim means "double fruitfulness."

Sometimes we have to forget the pain of our past to step into double fruitfulness. God called me into the restaurant industry to grow me in trust, faithfulness, and fruitfulness. All the pain of the years of brokenness, drugs, and being lost were slowly washed away like the tide. When God restores, it is greater than the original.

MARKETPLACE MINISTRY

When I first bought the restaurant, God led me to forget the pain of my previous life and just to focus on serving with excellence and fruitfulness. I read the parable of the Wedding Feast, and was touched so deeply. I decided to follow Jesus and try to simply do "his letters in red." I read the Scripture about the Parable of the Wedding Feast. I believe true financial prosperity is when money simply allows one to obey God and pursue the dreams in your heart.

A BANQUET TABLE FOR THE POOR

Feeding The Poor

But when you are invited, go and sit down in the lowest place, so that when he who invited you comes he may say to you, 'Friend, go up higher.' Then you will have glory in the presence of those who sit at the table with you. For whoever exalts himself will be humbled, and he who humbles himself will be exalted. Then He also said to him who invited Him, "When you give a dinner or a supper, do not ask your friends, your brothers, your relatives, nor rich neighbors, lest they also invite you back, and you will be repaid. But when you give a feast, invite the poor, the maimed, the lame, the blind. And you will be blessed, because they cannot repay you; for you shall be repaid at the resurrection of the just." (Luke 14:10-14)

When I read this Scripture, I wanted to follow the letters in red which Jesus instructed us to do. It is not just about having faith but really pressing in for the faith of God.

God opened the door to meet the president of The Springfield Rescue Mission, a local homeless ministry near my hometown. I got to tour the mission which was an old 1800's building nestled in downtown Springfield. I climbed up the old attic in the Springfield Rescue Mission and discovered his wife sorting through mountains of clothes to give away. She looked like Mrs. Claus preparing presents for all the children.

God gave me a prophetic dream to help. The Lord led me to sow into three separate local ministries: The Springfield Rescue Mission, My Father's House (both of which cater to the needs of homeless men), and Hope for Kids (A ministry dedicated to helping inner city youth). I would love to set a feast prepared for kings -- lobster bisque, piping hot prime rib and the best of the best for these princes and princesses. Other times, I would give them an open menu to order whatever their hearts desired. I would prepare meals for the graduates of the missions and I loved seeing Jesus in each and every one of them. It was like The Lord Jesus Himself would smile back, thanking me.

BUILDING MY TRUST IN GOD

I used to live solely for me. But now as a Christian, I had to learn to live for Him alone and to lay down my life for others. I was no longer earning large sums of money in my marijuana selling business, and I had to pay my employees and fully cover the overhead of the restaurant. God taught me profound lessons in this season to grow my trust in Him to provide. He knows every detail of our businesses and our lives. Every hair of our head is numbered!

Many of us are hesitant to talk about money and even squirm at the thought of it being brought up in church. Maybe you have been wounded by feeling used for money, bad beliefs and theology, or prosperity preachers. Many mock the televangelists who manipulate people's money, but we cannot throw out the baby with the bathwater.

In my early days as a young Christian, I simply could not eat enough of God's Word. The more I ate, the hungrier I got. I started to listen to God TV to feed my spirit. I remember one night, Benny Hinn came on the show. He was having a fatherly conversation with his son-in-law, Michael Koulianos. Benny then started sharing about always giving God a sacrifice which costs us.

IF IT DOESN'T MOVE YOU, IT DOESN'T MOVE GOD

"David replied to Araunah, 'No. I'm buying it from you, and at the full market price. I'm not going to offer GOD sacrifices that are no sacrifice.'" (1 Chronicles 21:24-27, The Message)

The Lord instructed me to sow extravagantly and give Him a sacrifice which costs a lot. I decided to give up to the point where it was uncomfortable. The Lord told me to empty out any money I had nefariously made and sow it into the kingdom. The Bible promises that He will transfer the wealth of the wicked into the kingdom.

I drove to the post office on a Sunday when it was closed. I rolled down the window. I took out a check which would clear out whatever I had left. I dropped the check into the mail. No one saw this moment but God. Truly, we live before an audience of One.

The sound of cheering filled my car like cheerleaders in a stadium. It was like heaven was cheering me on, as The Father saw me give my seed of sacrifice. One chapter of my life was closing, and a new day was dawning. I could not afford to take the past into the present. There could be no rearview mirror. I was forgetting the past and pressing forward on a fast track from heaven to quickly step into what God created me to be. And He sent me the perfect partner to walk with me step by step this side of eternity.

TITHING FROM THE RESTAURANT

Generosity Encouraged

"Remember this: Whoever sows sparingly will also reap sparingly, and whoever sows generously will also reap generously. Each of you should give what you have decided in your heart to give, not reluctantly or under compulsion, for God loves a cheerful giver. And God is able to bless you abundantly, so that in all things at all times, having all that you need, you will abound in every good work." (2 Corinthians 9:6-8)

As a newborn Christian who was building a new business, finances were tight. I heard about a minister who had neglected to tithe. He owed about $17,000 in tithes. He emptied their bank account to fulfill the neglected tithe. Days later, they received their largest offering of $17,000 -- the exact amount he sowed.

Hearing his testimony, this growing conviction hit me as I realized that I had not been tithing either with what I was making at the restaurant. I knew that I needed to give the tithe I'd never sowed. If I chose to obey and pay back what was owed to God, it would empty my bank account to a nerve-racking low level. How could I do this when so many families depended on me for income? How could I trust God to take care of me and then also their families?

THE WIDOW'S MITE

The Father led me to read the lesson of the widow's mite in Mark 12:41-44 and Luke 21:1-4. I marveled how the widow sowed and gave her mite which was a huge sacrifice for her. Jesus did not actually care about the money but about her heart.

If the widow could sow, so could I! So, I sowed what I owed God in tithes and believed in faith for God to come through! The deadline awaited for payroll and bills. That week, my business slowed down to a snail's pace. On Saturday night, we had the most incredible record-breaking night at the restaurant, and God brought in everything I needed in one evening.

I thought that maybe my lesson to trust in God for finances was done. Surely, I had passed the test, right? I had determined to always tithe at least 20%. But it was years and a long season, where the Lord always brought in what we needed -- but often at 11:59.

God loves a cheerful giver. *"Now He who supplies seed to the sower and bread for food will also supply and increase your store of seed and will enlarge the harvest of your righteousness."* (2 Cor. 9:10) He is the One who gives the seed! The Father knows every single detail in our lives, our families and our bank accounts. He truly has the whole world in His hand. He knows what needs to be paid and when. He is the ultimate CPA.

PROBLEMS BECOME OPPORTUNITY FOR SOLUTIONS

"Trust in the LORD with all your heart, And lean not on your own understanding; In all your ways acknowledge Him, And He shall direct your paths." (Proverbs 3:5-6)

God took me on a long journey to show me my job was not my provider, He was. After years of building this muscle of trust, God finally brought me into a place where I could just rest, trusting my Father.

WEEKLY PRAYER MEETINGS
AT THE RESTAURANT

In about 2013, the Lord stirred my heart to start a weekly prayer meeting on Monday at 7am in the restaurant. I invited brothers in the Lord. The prayer meeting lasted about 90 minutes. The Lord taught me how I could transform the marketplace into a ministry center. Sanctuaries do not just have to be formal houses of prayer. Wherever we are, He is there.

I would sit and listen to people's hearts, stories, and we would lay hands on each other and minister to one another. And see God's hand move upon their lives.

DO NOT DESPISE THE DAY
OF SMALL BEGINNINGS

"For who has despised the day of small things?" (Zechariah 4:10)

The Lord really built faithfulness and fruitfulness in this season of owning my restaurant for nine years. A lot of restaurants do "two sets of books" to hide cash. The Lord would not allow me to do this. I knew in my heart that I had to be honest. He always sees what we do in secret.

CATCH THE LITTLE FOXES

"Catch for us the foxes, the little foxes that ruin the vineyards, our vineyards that are in bloom." (Song of Songs 2:15)

One day, an employee wanted me to pay him in cash for the week so he could earn extra money. I told him I would do it, but just once. The Lord would strongly correct me if I tried to hide money or pay employees in cash. He was growing a sensitivity to the Holy Spirit in me. I was growing daily in my conviction about even the smallest compromises.

Then I made a promise to the Lord and also publicly to my staff that everything in my business was on the books. I learned to depend on God to put the perfect dream team as my staff. I also learned to trust The Father even in disasters.

SNOW IN OCTOBER

I have an incredible testimony of when we operate naturally in the supernatural, and God uses us in that Goshen principle to feed others even during famine.

In New England, we have gorgeous towering oak trees. One year, we had an early snow storm in October, the weight of the snow knocked down many of the trees and power lines. There was no power for an entire week. Even the restaurants lost power. The lights started flickering in my restaurant, and I began to pray, "Lord, don't let the power go out!"

He answered that prayer! All the restaurants in my town lost power – except for mine. I was the only one who had food in my town at my restaurant. Shelves were empty in all the grocery stories, but I was able to get food from Rhode Island. One of my favorite Psalms is Psalms 23 because *"The Lord is my Shepherd I shall not want."*

God wants us to learn to look to Him who is above all banks, weather patterns, kings, or governments. We are created to always have more than enough. We are created according to John 10:10 to have life abundantly. What does it look like to have all things added to you?

FEEDING THE MULTITUDES

"But remember the LORD your God, for it is he who gives you the ability to produce wealth, and so confirms his covenant, which he swore to your ancestors, as it is today." (Deuteronomy 8:18)

We have the power to produce wealth! God connected me with a ministry in a gang-riddled area where the gangs would target young kids in school to try to lure them into gang life. God has given me a heart for the youth. Once a month, I fed two or three hundred youth during their outreach at the school while I had the restaurant.

I loved feeding the homeless in Northampton. One of the churches allowed these men and women to sleep in their church to escape the cold, and I would cook a beautiful spread for them. The meals were so good that when the overseers saw how delectable they were, they also wanted to eat.

We are created to partner with God. He has visions for our lives, and He gives the provisions. We are created to display the glory of God within us! I will end this section by sharing a favorite passage from a favorite version of the Bible.

"I am convinced that any suffering we endure is less than nothing compared to the magnitude of glory that is about to be unveiled within us. The entire universe is standing on tiptoe, yearning to see the unveiling of God's glorious

sons and daughters! For against its will the universe itself has had to endure the empty futility resulting from the consequences of human sin. But now, with eager expectation, all creation longs for freedom from its slavery to decay and to experience with us the wonderful freedom coming to God's children." (Romans 8:18-21 TPT)

Feeding the community was a tradition that started at my grandparents' restaurant.

Chapter 10
Unforgiveness is Like Drinking Poison and Expecting the Other Person to Die

"A man's wisdom gives him patience; it is his glory to overlook an offense." (Proverbs 19:11)

"Love is to not be easily angered and to keep no record of wrong." (1 Corinthians 13:5)

To overlook an offense could be the primary indicator that a believer is walking in high levels of spiritual maturity. One definition of "overlooking" is: "to take no notice of, or to allow an offense to go unpunished." There is a famous quote about how we "judge ourselves by our intentions and others by their behavior." We all too often have a double standard and are quick to want to punish others; yet, we believe we deserve the benefit of a doubt. We accept the reckless love of God for ourselves but do not offer it as freely to others. But love holds no record of wrongs.

Joseph chose to forgive and overlook past offenses. I think this was Joseph's single greatest attribute and why God chose him to deliver a nation.

The shortage of food in Canaan forced Jacob to send his sons to buy grains from the Egyptians. Rachel only had two sons, Joseph and Benjamin. Jacob feared he would lose Benjamin as he had lost his beloved Joseph and he did not allow him to travel to Egypt with the brothers.

JOSEPH'S BROTHERS DON'T RECOGNIZE HIM

When Joseph finally encountered his brothers again, he concealed his identity. Scripture states that when Joseph's brothers first stood before him in Egypt, they did not even realize it was their beloved lost brother whom they had sold into slavery thirteen years before: *"Joseph recognized his brothers, but they did not recognize him."* (Genesis 42:8)

Light belongs in the darkness! Joseph, however, demonstrated his ability and his integrity even being in a leadership position. Imagine this epic scene! Joseph accused his brothers of being spies and told them to return with Benjamin, or he would not sell them grain. The ongoing famine forced Jacob to reluctantly send his sons back to Egypt with Benjamin. In Egypt, they were unexpectedly invited to dine at Joseph's house.

SECOND TEST

Joseph then tested the character of his brothers by placing a silver cup in the sack of Benjamin, falsely accusing him of theft. When Judah offered to stay in place of Benjamin, Joseph knew deep down in his heart that after all these years and tears, his brothers were truly changed men. Their character had transformed. This deeply moved Joseph to the point of tears. Holding back his tears, he finally revealed who he was! What an epic scene of redemption and reconciliation.

GOD MEANT IT FOR GOOD

Upon discovering Joseph's identity, his brothers were sure he would yield his imperial powers to exact revenge against them for their evil conduct, but Joseph explained they need not feel guilty for betraying him, as it was God's plan for him to be in Egypt to preserve his family. He told them to bring their father and his entire household into Egypt to live in the province of Goshen because there were five more years of famine left. Joseph supplied them with Egyptian transportation of wagons, new garments, silver, and twenty additional donkeys carrying provisions for the journey. Jacob was then joyously reunited with his son Joseph. Joseph's story highlights the power of forgiveness!

GOD WORKS IT ALL FOR GOOD

Joseph recognized that all the trials he had undergone were ordained to ensure the survival of Egypt and the surrounding countries. Keeping this in mind enabled him to forgive his brothers and repay evil with benevolence.

Joseph looked to God and His divine storyline:

Thus you shall say to Joseph: "I beg you, please forgive the trespass of your brothers and their sin; for they did evil to you." "Now, please, forgive the trespass of the servants of the God of your father." And Joseph wept when they spoke to him. Then his brothers also went and fell down before his face, and they said, "Behold, we are your servants." Joseph said to them, "Do not be afraid, for am I in the place of God? But as for you, you meant evil against me; but God meant it for good, in order to bring it about as it is this day, to save many people alive." (Genesis 50:17-20)

TO THE ONE WHO HAS BEEN FORGIVEN MUCH, LOVES MUCH

About two years after the trial, many of my friends witnessed the radical work of transformation in my life. It was only through the grace of God that I was able to change. One of my favorite stories in the Bible is about Mary of Bethany who throws herself at Jesus and anoints His feet with a year's wages of costly perfume. (Luke 7)

The one who has been forgiven much, loves much. I had received so much of the mercy and grace of God, God gave me grace to extend that to others. Many friends did not understand why I was not infuriated at the many people who ratted me out and testified against me. Even when Dennis Crame prophesied over me, he recounted how The Lord thanked me for not taking on bitterness, resentment, being angry at God, or any other destructive mindset which drives a wedge in our relationship with God. God sees our hearts and takes note of it all.

The arrest was truly a turning point in my life. I do not think I would have had the willpower and self control to walk away from this lifestyle if I had not been forced to stop. This had to happen because my struggle with living between two worlds would have never ended. God snatched **me** from my own path of destruction.

"Enter through the narrow gate, for wide is the gate and broad is the road that leads to destruction, and many enter through it. But small is the gate and narrow the road that leads to life, and only a few find it." (Matthew 7:13-14)

A BUBBLE OF GRACE

Even when I was going through the eighteen months of the trial, I was never mad at my accusers. Not that this was fun! It was incredibly stressful.

In the end, when all was settled, I had to pay $650,000! The FBI had listed the many agencies that investigated my case and how much money was allocated to each agency.

It took giving up everything I had to find Him. Jim Elliot, the famous missionary to Ecuador who was killed by a remote tribe of Indians wrote: *"He is no fool who gives what he cannot keep to gain what he cannot lose."*

Jesus is the only One who could fill the void in my heart and nothing else could satisfy. Friends who had never experienced the Lord really struggled to understand. Now, I was truly satisfied because the void was filled. I finally had peace which transcends all understanding. Jesus truly is the only Way, the Truth, and the Life.

ONCE AN ENEMY, NOW A BROTHER IN CHRIST

One day, I was at a men's conference at a local church. Believers from all over the region gathered to worship together and share God's Word. One of the guest speakers was an African American man. As he approached the stage, I suddenly remembered that he was the US Marshall who investigated me for the months leading up to my arrest. In fact, he was the lead investigator for my case.

At the end of the conference, this US Marshall was in a rush to catch a plane, but I was excited to speak to him before he left.

As I approached him, I could not wait to tell him the good news. I introduced myself to him. He knew exactly who I was, and he even remembered the address where I grew the pot – it was as if it had happened yesterday. When I began to thank him for doing his job, he looked surprised. My words of appreciation seemed to melt through the tough facade of the US Marshall. He maintained his professional composure, but I was probably the only convict who had thanked him for doing his job to have me arrested.

In God's divine order, he had been used to bring me back to life. In those brief moments we had a great conversation. When God restores, it is greater than the original. We truly are trophies of God's grace.

I find it ironic that during the time that he hunted me down, he was also my brother in the Lord. The US Marshall was actually answering my prayers without me knowing it. God was using him to bring me to my knees. Years later, I was a new man – thanks in part to him. Only God could weave our stories together so masterfully. As we worshiped together in one accord, the Lord was preparing us for all eternity together with Him. God can even use those who we think are our enemies – like Joseph's brothers - in the divine timeline of our story in God. Like Bill Johnson says, *"God even wins with a deck of twos."*

WE FORGIVE FOR THE SAKE OF OUR OWN HEARTS

Forgiveness can be the most difficult thing for most people to do. There are spiritual implications when we choose to hold onto bitterness and not offer a free gift to forgive. Even in the face of the most horrific traumas, we can choose to forgive. We radically do this for the sake of our own hearts – not others. Matthew 6:15 warns us: *"But if you do not forgive others their sins, your Father will not forgive your sins."*

This world is not our home. There will always be a price to pay while we are here on earth. And there are spiritual laws that are applied at the same time – forgiveness is one of them.

BE ANGRY BUT DO NOT SIN

I want to take a moment to validate your pain or even your anger. What happened to you may not be excusable - we do not simply sweep it under the rug. You can forgive the sinner without excusing or nullifying the sin.

There is a difference between forgiveness and reconciliation. Even if you have every right to be angry at your perpetrator, we as believers have to rise up in this upside-down kingdom. Jesus is our example. He died, so we could live.

When we realize how much we need His mercy, we are slower to withhold mercy to others. When we are aware of our own need for the cross, it is easier to lavish forgiveness on our brothers and sisters who are earthenware vessels just like us. We can make a powerful choice to forgive those who have hurt us! We forgive their trespasses simply because we were freely forgiven by the One who knows us best and loves us most. This definitely is not a natural instinct. But it is a spiritual law like gravity – when we choose to forgive, we ourselves become free.

GOD GIVES GRACE TO FORGIVE

As Matthew 5 reads, we are called to settle the matter quickly, before our adversary takes us to court. I imagine unforgiveness like walking around shackled with a ball and chain around you. It is pretty hard to move forward when you are dragging around the pain of the past.

When you actually open your mouth by a free act of your will to choose to release those who have hurt you into the freedom of forgiveness, then the chains will begin to fall off of you. This will also help them to receive their own healing, too. The Father faithfully forgives you, and you receive His forgiveness.

We must be both quick to forgive and also quick to receive forgiveness. There is a difference between conviction and condemnation. Satan accuses us night and day. When we learn to live from grace, we can freely extend that same grace to others.

DON'T JUST FORGIVE - BLESS YOUR ENEMIES

Therefore, if you are offering your gift at the altar and there remember that your brother or sister has something against you, leave your gift there in front of the altar. First go and be reconciled to them; then come and offer your gift. "Settle matters quickly with your adversary who is taking you to court. Do it while you are still together on the way, or your adversary may hand you over to the judge, and the judge may hand you over to the officer, and you may be thrown into prison. Truly I tell you, you will not get out until you have paid the last penny. {Matthew 5:23-26)

It is not enough to just forgive. The Bible commands us to then pray a blessing upon them. Another key step is to forgive yourself. In doing this the chains will be broken off of you, and you will not be in bondage. Another key step is to first repent to God for your own unforgiveness against others, against God, or even against yourself. By choosing to forgive yourself and others you will start to heal. Here is another key Scripture:

"Be kind and compassionate to one another, forgiving each other, just as in Christ God forgave you." (Ephesians 4:32)

Jesus left the right-hand side of the Father in heaven and clothed Himself in flesh to redeem all of mankind. Though He once possessed all riches in heaven, Jesus became the ultimate missionary by coming to earth and becoming fully man. Jesus never asks us to do anything that He has not already done. As a man, He chose to forgive, and therefore, we are without excuse to withhold forgiveness to others.

While Jesus hung on the cross with the two thieves on either side, he chose to forgive. He was not angry at the ones who mocked and tortured him. We must learn to respond as He did:

As He hung on the cross, Jesus said, *"Father, forgive them, for they do not know what they are doing." And they divided up his clothes by casting lots."* (Luke 23:34) If Jesus could forgive us, we have no right to withhold forgiveness towards others.

NELSON MANDELA

Nelson Mandela was unjustly imprisoned for twenty-seven years in colonial prison in South Africa after decades of apartheid. After apartheid ended, he was elected as President. The very first person he invited to his inaugural address was the former warden where he was imprisoned. This warden was the very person who called for Nelson Mandela's death sentence. He chose to honor the one who wanted him dead!

He was tortured over many of the years he spent in prisoned. However, when he was finally released in 1990, he called not for revenge – but for forgiveness and reconciliation.

Many felt betrayed that he would turn away from righteous anger. Nelson Mandela embodied the beauty of a love which holds no records of wrongs (1 Corinthians 13). The world took note of such a powerful heart and mind, and thus, it came to be that the dark years of apartheid reached their end. God had healed his heart so fully he was able to have compassion on his enemies.

WALKING OUT A FREE MAN

As he said in his own words, *"As I walked out the door toward the gate that would lead to my freedom, I knew if I didn't leave my bitterness and hatred behind, I'd still be in prison."*

Come follow us on the narrow path to an abundant life.

Chapter 11
Leaving a Legacy for Your Children & Children's Children

"We were like those who dream [it seemed so unreal]. Then our mouth was filled with laughter And our tongue with joyful shouting; Then they said among the nations, "The LORD has done great things for them." The LORD has done great things for us; We are glad!" (Psalms 126:2-3 Amplified, emphasis, mine)

During Covid-19, the worship anthem that rang throughout America was "The Blessing" by Kari Jobe, Cody Carnes, Chris Brown and Steven Furtick reminding us that we are all God's dream, and His favor goes to a thousand generations.

Family was God's idea. We are His family. Family is His unit to express the covenantal unity between Father, Son and Holy Spirit. He calls us to fight for our family just like He fought for us to be His family with Him forever, by laying down His life in love. *"Behold, children are a heritage and gift from the LORD, The fruit of the womb a reward. Like arrows in the hand of a warrior, So are the children of one's youth."* (Psalms 127:3-4 AMP)

WHOLE FAMILIES WILL CHANGE THE WORLD

"After I looked things over, I stood up and said to the nobles, the officials and the rest of the people, 'Don't be afraid of them. Remember the Lord, who is great and awesome, **and fight for your families,** *your sons and your daughters, your wives and your homes.' When our enemies heard that we were aware of their plot and that God had frustrated it."* (Nehemiah 4:14-15)

We are called to fight for our family. We are all just broken people invited onto holy ground. The good news of the gospel of Jesus Christ is that the Father welcomes us all home. Prodigals are simply trophies of His grace. My life is a sign and a wonder that if God can use me, how much more can He use you! The Father is not surprised by your weakness. He does not disqualify or disown us even when others in the Body of Christ might be embarrassed by us. We are all redeemed, forgiven, chosen, anointed, and appointed.

As Heidi Baker says, *"We are all just little earthenware jars of clay in the dirt."* Jesus is the only treasure. We just contain Him. His light shines brightest through the shattered shards of our own heartbreak and struggle.

My testimony should be an invitation to you – If the Father can redeem Mark Danalis, you all stand without excuse. If God can prophesy through a donkey, He can use us all. My highest ceiling should be a launching pad for you. Just reach out your hand. One touch of His garment, and we will never be the same. He is willing, and He is able.

Sit with the forgiven. Walk with the family of God. Rest in the arms of your Heavenly Father. May my story compel you. We are all part of His masterpiece of redemption and reconciliation. I think the greatest miracle this side of eternity is seeing our children and children's children love the Lord. To me, it is more miraculous than raising the dead. We get to pay a price today for a generation we may never even meet (if the Lord tarries)." Our righteous choices today rewrite our own history in love and determine the destinies of our children. We break generational curses, and we release blessings. Our battles today ensure our children's victories tomorrow.

Heaven is not a singular experience, but a communal experience of thousands of generations worshiping the Lamb around the throne and fellowshipping together. There is a power of generational inheritance. The Great Cloud of witnesses are all cheering you on today. They are peering over the balcony of heaven in the culmination of the ages asking you to take your place in the processional of history. Will you become Jesus' glorious inheritance? Will you give Him your full "yes?" Your simple obedience impacts all of eternity.

Healthy families will change the world. Live aware of His presence. Embrace His Word so deeply that we meditate on it continuously; its evidence through our confession and our decree. It positions us to pray for things that shape the course of world history.

We can change the course of human history just like Joseph. And we can also change the trajectory of our own family, too. Our greatest revenge to the enemy is to shift our family line into God's divine timeline. That is why I love the story of Joseph. God restored Joseph, and then used him as a catalyst to heal and save his own family. And then God used Joseph to deliver God's family - the nation of Israel.

JOSEPH WAS A PROTOTYPE

As we finish the last chapter of our book, Joseph is reunited with his beloved father, Jacob. Joseph ruled Egypt for a total of eighty years until his death at the age of one hundred and ten years old. Before his passing, he made his brothers promise to take his body with them when they would eventually leave Egypt for the Promised Land.

Before Jacob's death, he gave Joseph a gift: his children would be the only ones from among Jacob's grandsons to be treated as independent tribes.

After his death, he was embalmed and laid to rest in Egypt. Moses made sure to locate Joseph's tomb and carry his remains to the Land of Israel. Joseph was subsequently buried in Shechem.

REVIVAL LOOKS LIKE FAMILY

Even Joseph's two children, Manasseh and Ephraim, were blessed by Jacob and received land with the other ten tribes. I think the greatest measure of a transformed life is how much it affects our children. I wanted to share the miracles of how God not only broke all the generational curses in my life, but set my own children as double portions of the goodness of God in the land of the living. We must carry the baton and pass it off to the next generation. I would like to share the testimonies of my biological children, my beloved wife, and my spiritual daughter:

MY SON's TESTIMONY: THE PIVOT POINT

As I was graduating high school without any future plans, my father, Mark, sat me down at the restaurant he owned. I'd been familiar with this talk at this point in my life; hearing everyone's well meaning but often misguided opinions about what I should do after graduation. That day, my father said something different.

My father said to me "Whatever you decide to do, I will support you, but I want to read you something first." Then, he read Matthew 6:33: *"But seek first the kingdom of God and his righteousness, and all these things will be added to you."*

I replied "I have no idea what that means!"

"Ask God what your purpose is and then do it." This five-minute conversation at a restaurant that no longer exists today changed the trajectory of my life forever.

For three months, I would read a verse in the Bible each day (if I remembered) and pray, "Show me what you want me to do and I'll do it."

One day after several months, I felt led to go to a ministry school over one thousand miles away. This was a big step because I did not love to attend church. After all, my upbringing didn't exactly scream 'goody two shoes.' However, my father's words rang in my head, "Ask God what to do and then do it."

While at this ministry school, I was in the Word, studying, praying, and learning to love and serve others. I did not even realize that I was walking out this verse, *"Seek first the kingdom of God and His righteousness."* As you grow with God, you'll experience that His Word does not come back void and "all these things will be added to you."

I ended up meeting my incredible wife at this ministry school. God added so much to my life that I still feel overwhelmed by His goodness.

We all have pivot points in life. Sometimes a pivot point is a massive wakeup call: for my father, it was an arrest, a death, and a divorce. For me, it was a simple conversation with my dad in an empty restaurant. Part of the beauty of God is every day He offers you a pivot point – a fresh start or a new day with a clean slate. Ask God what to do and then do it.

"The steadfast love of the Lord never ceases, his mercies never come to an end; they are new every morning; great is your faithfulness." (Lamentations 3:22-23)

MY DAUGHTER BEATS CANCER

My daughter had her own pivot point in her life that was as dramatic as my son's. At the young age of twenty-two years old, she was diagnosed with Non-Hodgkin's Lymphoma stage 2B. The entire family was beyond shocked, as we did not know anyone her age with cancer.

Months earlier, when she was at an all-time personal low, she made the decision to pray the sinner's prayer to accept Jesus as her Lord and Savior.

Even though she had welcomed Jesus into her heart, her life was not miraculously better, nor was she instantly healed. But what was truly miraculous was that the Holy Spirit used this painful process to draw her into the loving arms of her Heavenly Father. She had never felt closer to Jesus and experienced a peace that blanketed her heart and mind that surpassed her own understanding. The Father never left her, and she never questioned why it was happening to her.

Before she had started treatment, she had considered an alternative holistic plan: doing a macrobiotic diet and attending The Kushi Institute; ultimately, she chose a traditional path of chemotherapy. Three months in, a PET scan had revealed the cancer was suddenly gone. The doctor recommended she finish the treatment plan and protocol, but she had made the decision to implement the holistic diet she had already been researching to ensure her remission. Her oncologist gave her his blessing with the agreement she would continue monthly blood work to monitor her progress.

In the medical world, after a year of clean testing, you are officially in remission. For the next twelve months, she strictly followed a personalized macrobiotic diet plan created by the Kushi Institute: no meat, sugar, dairy, processed foods, gluten, and all organic. This new way of living revolutionized her life.

FOOD CAN BE OUR MEDICINE – NOT OUR POISON

After a year, she was completely in remission and has been completely cancer free since! Food can be our medicine instead of our poison. She was not only healed, but now shares with others that they, too, have the power to help heal themselves.

Sometimes our greatest challenges become our ministry. She had faced death. Sharing her journey encourages and provides hope to others facing similar circumstances. Ten years later, she is now in the process of opening a cold pressed juice business, True Vine Juice Company, a company that will continue to share the message of the power of clean, healthy food and how it can help restore our bodies.

Jesus never promises that our lives become perfect after salvation, or that nothing bad will ever happen. Jesus actually warns us of the opposite of how in this life we will have tribulation but we can be of good courage. During her season of cancer, the Holy Spirit became her Comforter. He never once failed her. She was able to walk through the valley of the shadow of death and realize it is only a shadow (Psalms 23). Even at her darkest moments, Jesus became everything.

MY WIFE ELAINE

My wife Elaine has become my greatest cheerleader! Not only has she stood by me in the mountains, but she has comforted my heart in the deepest valleys. God has downloaded an incredible revelation to her about using clean healthy fruits and vegetables to help heal the body like medicine.

In Ezekiel 47, there were trees by the River of God which were fruitful twelve months of the year. The leaves were for the healing of the nations. God has spoken so clearly to her to be on a plant-based diet. I thought I was a professional cook, but she is really the gourmet chef of the family. She has learned how to cook everything from scratch, using different fruits and vegetables to support the body in its God given ability to heal itself. She tries to cook gluten-free, dairy-free, organic and vegan. Her cooking inspires others to start eating healthier.

At sixty-two years old, she is at the gym six days a week. I feel like she is growing younger. She is in the best shape of her life and a sign and a wonder of reverse aging. God is inviting us to return back to the Garden of Eden. We can walk with Him, talk with Him face to face and enjoy this beautiful playground of His presence we call planet earth.

I HAVE A DREAM...

I have a dream to establish Goshens like Joseph did, with supernatural gardens with a surplus of food for the healing of the nations even when there is famine and shakings. I know God wants us to be connected with the One who is the Source of everything.

"Then God said, 'Let the land burst forth with growth: plants that bear seeds of their own kind, and every variety of fruit tree, each with power to multiply from its own seed.' And so it happened. The land flourished with grasses, Every variety of seed-bearing plant, and trees bearing fruit with their seeds in them. And God loved what he saw, for it was beautiful." (Genesis 1:11-12)

God wants to restore everything that has been stolen from us, and He wants us to walk and talk with Him in our relationship with Him, just as Adam and Eve walked and talked with God in the garden. All of heaven rejoices, spins around, twirls and is so excited about YOU! God wants you to prosper in every way - spirit, soul and body! The Father is extravagant with joy and wants to lavish us in love. He throws a huge party in heaven with the angels the day each sinner is saved. Jesus came to not only get you into heaven but to get heaven into you before you die.

You can live from a heavenly perspective. Do you want to live a life greater than yourself which leaves a legacy for the next generation like my heart for my son and daughter? One of my greatest joys is now pouring into the next generation. I wanted to include the testimony of my spiritual daughter, Vanessa:

VANESSA'S STORY

I met Mark from church during a time when I was searching for community and family with whom I could share the love of Christ. Honestly, I was struggling with identity and my walk with the Lord. Mark was one of the friendliest and most inviting people I have ever met. When I first arrived at our church where he served, he immediately invited me to a youth group. This was very pivotal for me.

Mark had really been helping me with my walk: praying with me, inviting me to church events, pouring the Father's love into me, encouraging, and leading me to the Father's heart. For my entire life, I had struggled so much with my own sense of identity, having financial stability, and knowing both my purpose and gifts. Mark has always been there like a spiritual father, encouraging me to step into who God has called me to be.

Social media is a platform I know that I have been called to! Comparison and competition are such a thief of joy. I had been battling with thinking my story was not worthy enough to share. Mark always spoke truth over me, prayed with me, and has always encouraged me to follow my God-given dreams.

Throughout this period in my life, the Lord has brought me young women to mentor, and Mark has always been a spiritual father that I first consult with and ask for advice and prayer for. He is always, always there for God's children. I truly look up to him and the way he serves Christ. He always reminds me that the true riches of Christ are what matters most. He has been the hands and feet of Jesus to me.

FAMILY IS THE GOVERNMENT OF GOD

Raising spiritual or biological children correctly brings spiritual dividends to our entire spiritual lines. Our children are on loan from God. It is our responsibility to steward them in a way that is pleasing to The Father. We owe the world to do better than what we were given. We want to raise righteous and happy children.

I want to encourage you and invite you: Live your life in a way which impacts your children and children's children. As followers of Jesus, we live with the awareness and revelation that our Father is eternal, and has grafted us into His eternal kingdom. Our lives have a ripple effect, impacting all of eternity.

HISTORY WILL SPEAK KINDLY OF YOU

Winston Churchill said, *"History will speak kindly of you, for you are writing it."* In light of this, we must live consciously that what we do will be handed down to the next generation. Our 'yes' to the Lord matters. Our obedience impacts our own individual lives. But then, it goes down like the root of a tree that will bear fruit for the generations to come – far beyond our own lifetime.

THE INVITATION: IF GOD CAN USE ME...

I was saved in a dark, dirty jail cell, as a broken, drug-dealing sinner. Only in God's economy can God treasure what people reject. Only The Father can redeem my life and use it for the glory and the fame of His name. I boast in my own weakness and pray it encourages you.

Our Heavenly Father wants this last chapter not to be a closing, but a launching pad for you to propel you to dare to dream! What He has done in my life in the pages of this book, He wants to do exceedingly, abundantly more for you. (Ephesians 3:20) The Father is more committed to you than you are to Him. He wants to birth your God-given purpose while you are here on earth. Only you can move His heart the way you do. Only you can live out your God dream. Only you can give Jesus your all! Time is short. Every moment is a present. We must seize the day, not miss a moment, and write our own story with Him. *"I cry out to God most high, to God who fulfills his purpose for me."* (Psalms 57:2) Do you feel like He is fulfilling His purpose in your life? Do you feel weary? Come to Him as you are. Do you feel broken? He can heal and put you together. Do you feel disqualified? He alone qualifies you. We boast in Him alone. Let my story be an encouragement to you. Jesus comes to seek and save the lost.

He delights in the underdog. He leaves the ninety-nine to chase the one. He is the Father of the comeback. In the end only His opinion matters.

Jesus is knocking on the door of your heart, if you do not know Him, this is a perfect time to come to the altar. He is waiting with His loving arms wide open. All of heaven is rejoicing when the lost children of God come back home. When Jesus endured the cross, you were the "joy set before Him" – He saw you. You are His inheritance! Come and receive Jesus as your Lord and Savior.

You may know of Him intellectually, but do you know Him in the intimate way that He wants you to know Him? Come to the altar and rededicate your life to the Lord.

IT'S TIME TO COME HOME TO FATHER

"For it is with your heart that you believe and are justified, and it is with your mouth that you profess your faith and are saved." (Romans 10:9)

As you are reading this, He is with you right now, and you can say a very simple prayer: *"Jesus, I know that I am a sinner. I open my heart wide open. I invite You to come into my heart and be the Lord of my life. I surrender my life to You and You alone. I give you permission to light up the deepest darkest parts of my soul because I want to be healed, delivered, and set free from my bondage. I want you to show me what my purpose is, my God-dream that you have woven in my heart, and let Your glory fall upon me. I ask for my spiritual language from heaven to come forth now. And I know that surely Your goodness and love will follow me all the days of my life, and I will dwell in the house of the Lord forever. Amen."*

I want to close this book like an altar call. I have an invitation for you to come forward. Come to the Father who is too good to not believe. The lyrics of this closing worship song is my prayer for each and every reader. I want you to encounter the God who is too good to not believe. I want you to meet our Father who works all things together for the good of those who love Him (Romans 8:28), and truly uses what the enemy intended for evil for our good. (Genesis 50:20)

TOO GOOD TO NOT BELIEVE
SONG BY BRANDON LAKE AND CODY CARNES

I've lived stories that have proved Your faithfulness.
I've seen miracles my mind can't comprehend.
And there is beauty in what I can't understand.
Jesus, it's You, Jesus, it's You.
I believe
You're the wonder-working God.
You're the wonder-working God.
All the miracles I've seen.
Too good to not believe.
You're the wonder-working God
And You heal because You love
Oh, the miracles we'll see
You're too good to not believe
Too good to not believe
Too good to not believe, oh-oh
And I can't resurrect a man with my own hands But just the mention of Your name can raise the dead (yeah) All the glory to the only One who can
Jesus, it's You, Jesus, it's You (come on)
Oh, I believe
You're the wonder-working God (yes, You are) You're the wonder-working God
All the miracles I've seen
Too good to not believe
You're the wonder-working God
And You heal because You love
We've seen cancer disappear
We've seen broken bodies healed

122

Don't you tell me He can't do it
Don't you tell me He can't do it
We've seen real life resurrection
We've seen mental health restored
Don't you tell me He can't do it
Don't you tell me He can't do it
We've seen families reunited
We've seen prodigals return (come home)
Don't you tell me He can't do it
Don't you tell me He can't do it (don't you ever tell me)
We've seen troubled souls delivered
We've seen addicts finally freed (finally freed)
Don't you tell me He can't do it
Don't you tell me He can't do it
We'll see cities in revival
Salvation flood the streets (come on)
Don't you tell me He can't do it
Don't you tell me He can't do it
We'll see glory fill the nations
Like the world has never seen
Don't you tell me He can't do it
'Cause I know that He can
Yes, I believe (I believe)
You're the wonder-working God (oh, You are, You are, You are)
You're the wonder-working God
Too good to not believe (too good, too good)...
Don't you ever stop believing
'Cause He's so, so good
So, so good

"All of Egypt came to Joseph to buy corn because the famine was great in all the lands." (painting by H. Horvath)

"...but whoever drinks of the water that I will give him will never be thirsty again. The water that I will give him will become in him a spring of water welling up to eternal life." John 4:14 ESV

* * * * *

About The Author

Mark's desire in life is to be a friend of God. He loves revelation, the Glory of God and impartation accompanied by a sharp prophetic edge. His testimony is that to one who has been forgiven much, loves much! Radically saved in a jail cell after a drug bust, his life testifies that no one is too far gone for the loving arms of The Father. Mark also enjoys mentoring youth, radically setting people free from bondage, and helping others hear the voice of God through dreams, visions, signs, and wonders.

Made in United States
Orlando, FL
02 December 2023

39933407R00085